D0777013

LOST BOY

MY STORY

GREG LAURIE
WITH ELLEN VAUGHN

Regal

From Gospel Light
Ventura, California, U.S.A.

Published by Regal
From Gospel Light
Ventura, California, U.S.A.
www.regalbooks.com
Printed in the U.S.A.

Library of Congress Cataloging-in-Publication Data
Laurie, Greg.
Lost boy : my story / Greg Laurie ; with Ellen Vaughn.
p. cm.
ISBN 978-0-8307-4578-4 (hard cover)
1. Laurie, Greg. 2. Evangelists—United States—Biography. I. Vaughn, Ellen Santilli. II. Title.
BV3785.L275A3 2008
280—dc22
[B]
2008000599

Rights for publishing this book outside the U.S.A. or in non-English languages are administered
by Gospel Light Worldwide, an international not-for-profit ministry. For additional information, please visit www.glww.org, email info@glww.org, or write to Gospel Light Worldwide,
1957 Eastman Avenue, Ventura, CA 93003, U.S.A.

To Stella and Stella

*Stella McDaniel, my grandmother, who took me
to church for the first time.*

*Stella Laurie, my granddaughter, who reminds me
that I must be as a child to enter God's kingdom.*

O GOD OF MY SALVATION!
EVEN IF MY FATHER AND MOTHER
ABANDON ME,
THE LORD WILL HOLD ME CLOSE.

PSALM 27:9-10

CONTENTS

FOREWORD
BY FRANKLIN GRAHAM

Greg Laurie and I met 20 years ago through a mutual friend, Dennis Agajanian. The moment I met Greg, I liked him. You can't help but like him. God's hand is on his life.

When I heard him preach for the first time, my heart rejoiced at the clear presentation of the gospel and God's Word. Through the years, I have spent a great deal of time with Greg. We have shared in ministry opportunities—pastor's conferences, crusades—and I have had the privilege of preaching for him at Harvest Christian Fellowship, the church he founded some 35 years ago.

To hear about Greg's childhood and teenage years—and the change that took place when he encountered Jesus Christ—demonstrates the miracle of a transformed life. God the Father had His eye on this lost boy. He was led out of a dysfunctional home and the dark drug culture and set on the path to peace with God. Nothing short of the hand of God could take Greg from a life of despair and make him one of the top pastors in America today.

Greg's life—where he came from and what he came through—is a picture of God's grace, protection and love for a lost boy—cynical of everything but searching for something. And when Greg found everything in Jesus Christ, he began searching for others who needed what he had found—the Savior.

Greg Laurie's autobiography, *Lost Boy*, will touch your heart in a profound way. I am proud to know him. And as you read these pages, you will also come to know Greg and the God that he serves.

Franklin Graham, President and CEO
Billy Graham Evangelistic Association
Samaritan's Purse

FOREWORD
BY CHUCK SMITH

It was late afternoon on a Monday. I had just finished my hour-long radio program during which I answer Bible questions from listeners who call in from all over the United States. As I left the studio, I found, waiting in the hallway, one of my special sons in the faith. Greg Laurie had a smile on his face and held a manuscript in his hand. Would I read it? Perhaps comment on it? Of course, he knew that he didn't even need to ask.

Later that night, after the dishes were done, I sat at the dinner table and began to read. I became absorbed in the story and lost all track of time. When my wife, Kay, called for me to come upstairs and go to bed, I glanced at my watch and discovered that it was 11:05 P.M. I had become so engrossed in the story that I had no idea it was that late. I had almost finished the manuscript, and I could not wait to get up early the next morning to finish the gripping story of God's wonderful grace.

As I read *Lost Boy*, my mind flashed back to the first time I met Greg back in the early '70s. My wife and I lived near Harbor High School in Newport Beach, and we often had visits from flower children of the hippie era. So when the bell rang and I opened the front door to see this long-haired young man standing there with a smile on his face and something for me to read in this hand, I was not surprised.

Greg handed me a comic strip that he had drawn. It was a graphic depiction of the sermon I had preached the previous Sunday—I had titled it "Living Water." The drawings impressed me, but even more remarkable was how he had taken the verbal message that he had heard and re-communicated it in such an interesting artistic form.

Immediately, I recognized the special talent of this young man and asked him to redraw the cartoon sequencing the pictures and stories so that we could print it as a small booklet that could be handed out to young people in schools and on the beaches. We printed 10,000 of these tracts and had a crew of kids staple them together. We set them out for the kids to take and to pass out to their friends.

The first night the Living Water tract was available, every copy disappeared—so we had 100,000 printed. The same thing happened. In a matter of days, every copy was gone. I do not know how many million copies of that tract were printed, but each one brought a message of hope to a lost boy or lost girl who furtively was searching for meaning in life through drugs, sex and other forms of pleasure.

Through the years, it has been a great blessing to watch how God took this lost boy, turned his life around and used him to touch so many others with a message of hope. As you read about Greg's childhood and teen years, you might naturally begin to wonder if anything good could come out of his crazy mixed-up dysfunctional home. You will be surprised and encouraged by God's answer.

Lost Boy is truly an exciting story of God's grace at work.

Chuck Smith
Senior Pastor, Calvary Chapel Costa Mesa

LOST BOY

A WORD OF EXPLANATION

Like most pastors, I'm a verbal kind of guy. Paragraphs, pages and sermons bubble out of my head and follow me wherever I go, and most of them end up in my books.

But this book is different from anything I've ever written before.

It's a story. My story.

Over the years I've shared parts of it, and I've often used personal experiences to illustrate biblical truths. But this is just the facts, ma'am. No devotional thoughts tied in, no biblical exegesis, no life applications.

Okay, maybe a few. But I'll do my best not to preach, though I may slip now and then.

What follows is just my story, about a kid who was lost and got found. A boy I used to know. I resonate with what comedian Steve Martin wrote in his memoir: "In a sense, this book is not an autobiography but a biography, because I am writing about someone I used to know. Yes, these events are true, yet sometimes they seemed to have happened to someone else, and I often felt like a curious onlooker or someone trying to remember a dream."[1]

This Greg I used to know came from pretty bad beginnings. He grew up to be a quirky adult with wild tales to tell. But the big story here isn't so much about the lost boy. It's about the great God who found him and would not let him go.

Helping me with this has been Ellen Vaughn, a gifted *New York Times* number-one bestselling author who has worked with Chuck Colson on many of his books. She is why this book is more of a compelling story than many of my previous works. Ellen is fairly quirky herself, which is why you'll see some pretty colorful anecdotes here and there that have never made it into my sermons—and most likely never will.

A disclaimer: Much of this book is drawn from my memories. But because memory is subjective and sometimes elusive, some might question how I've chosen to tell parts of my story. I have tried my best to recall the events as they happened. I've taken great care to double-check things with others when possible. But in the end, this is my story as best I can remember and tell it.

As I've reflected, I've remembered scenes I'd long forgotten—some of which I would have preferred to stay forgotten. I've thought about people I've known, some who are still right by my side today, and some who are dead and gone. I've seen dark and light strands woven together, times of pain I wish I hadn't had, and times of laughter so deep and huge that I smile when I remember . . . and the wild thing is, again, that this story isn't about me. It's about God . . . and how He uses absolutely everything, good and bad, to draw us to Himself and keep us there. Some of you know exactly what I mean, some don't. That's okay. When I began living out this story, I didn't have a clue either.

So if I had to boil this down to one word, I'd say it's a story of *hope* . . . and I really pray that through it, God's hope will break through to you like a tsunami.

Greg Laurie
Riverside, California
February 2, 2008

Note
1. Steve Martin, *Born Standing Up* (New York: Scribner, 2007), n.p.

THUMBNAIL SKETCHES

It's summer in Southern California, and I'm in the narrow walkway under Angel Stadium. I hear the muffled roar of 40,000 people yelling, clapping and stomping their feet, and the last crashing chords of the band's big finale.

It's deafening, but still distant. Every step draws me closer to the stairway that leads to the field and the immense stage. The band finishes its set and I hear applause, like the thunder of waves crashing on a rocky shore. It's time for the message of the evening, from Greg Laurie.

I emerge from the third-base dugout and run up a few more steps onto the stage platform, sweating a little in my black T-shirt. I grab both sides of the podium and look out over the big ball field into the arena of tens of thousands of human beings. It feels as if they are all looking toward me, expecting something exciting to happen, hoping I'll say something fascinating or enlightening.

At that moment, my brain breaks into split-screen mode.

On one side I'm the guy who's been the pastor of a big church for 30 years, the guy who speaks at crusades all over the world, the guy who preaches and teaches on radio and TV . . . and I can't wait to tell them about what God can really do in their lives.

On the other side of my mind thoughts flit around like gnats I can't quite catch. *Look at this huge stadium! I hope I don't disappoint these people. How did I end up here?*

Who in the world is Greg Laurie anyway?

*   *   *

It's a hot summer night in the mid-1960s in Honolulu, Hawaii. I'm 10 years old, wearing a white cotton T-shirt and pajama bottoms. I'm alone in our beautiful home overlooking Waikiki Beach. My mom is married to a guy named Eddie this time, and they've been out. I can't fall asleep until she gets home.

I don't look at the clock, but it's way past midnight when I finally hear the front door open. Then there's the familiar tinkle of ice cubes in glasses, the murmur of conversation, the slosh of more drinks being poured.

Then, like every night, the arguing starts. The volume rises. He yells something unprintable. She yells back. I hear an ashtray smash against the wall, and then the crash of more broken glass. Screaming.

I hunch in my bed like I always do, waiting for it to end, even praying a little, though I don't really know who I'm praying to. Now there's more cussing and yelling, and then I hear a dull thud that's somehow worse than everything that came before.

My stomach flips, and I get out of bed and run into the kitchen. My mom is lying limp on the floor, a puddle of red pooling under her platinum blonde hair. I've seen her passed out lots of times, but this is different.

Eddie is standing over her, breathing hard, a heavy, bloody wooden statue in his hand.

"She's okay," he says in a threatening tone. "It's just ketchup. Go back to your room! She's fine!"

He's an adult, and I'm a kid, but I know that's not ketchup. But I also know that he just might kill me, too, if I stay where I am.

"Okay," I say, backing down the hallway. "I'll just go back to bed."

I get back to my room and close the door. Then I run to the open window, pop out the screen, and fling my leg over the edge. It's not much of a drop to the ground. I sit on the sill, then push off and land hard on the grass, falling forward onto my hands. I jump up and run next door.

The neighbor's house is dark, but the windows are open. I pound hard on the front door, trying to be loud and quiet at the same time, terrified that Eddie will hear and come after me.

I'm panting, knocking so hard that my knuckles hurt. All I can think is that we've got to get an ambulance.

Finally, a light comes on and I hear someone calling.

"Who is it?"

"It's Greg!" I call, my voice shaking a little. "Greg Laurie!"

* * *

It's 1970. I've got Beatles posters on the walls of my room and a tab of orange sunshine in my system. I've been influenced by people like Timothy Leary—who tells me to "tune in, turn on, drop out"—and the other heroes of my generation, like Jimi Hendrix, Jim Morrison and Janis Joplin. I'm on my way to pulling off at least part of their creed: live fast, die young and leave a beautiful corpse.

But the LSD in my brain isn't pretty. I'm looking in the mirror, and all I see is melting flesh, drooping eyes, burning bones.

Is that me?

* * *

I'm a new father with a brand-new life. My wife is sweet and beautiful; we are young and have big dreams. Our son is a toddler. I never had a dad, so I want to protect my child in ways I was never protected. I can't believe how great it is to carry little Christopher around on my shoulders, to tickle him and hear him laugh. He has shining blond hair and bright brown eyes. He's curious and into everything.

One day, I'm distracted for just a moment while Christopher is playing on the floor in our bedroom. There's a narrow, heavy, full-length mirror leaning against the wall. I look up in time to see Christopher pulling the mirror toward himself . . . just in time to see it falling on top of him.

I scream and run for my son. Broken shards of daggered glass are everywhere, and Christopher is covered in blood.

"Daddy!" he cries. "Daddy!"

* * *

I am standing before an enormous polished mahogany table in an executive suite. It's a meeting of the board of directors for the Billy Graham Association. They represent hundreds of years of academic and theological training; dozens of degrees, awards and honors; millions of dollars of business success; and thousands of hours of counsel to people in need.

I have been nominated to become a member of this distinguished group. Before they vote me in or out, I've been asked to give a short talk. My friend Franklin Graham introduces me. As I speak, the most famous evangelist in human history is sitting before me, nodding a little, listening to every word. I don't know what Billy Graham is thinking just then, but I sure know what I'm thinking.

How in the world did I end up here?

* * *

The television studio is cold. I'm sitting across the desk from famed CNN interviewer Larry King. Larry is wearing his trademark suspenders, a crisp, teal-green collared shirt, and, much to my surprise, a pair of faded blue jeans . . . since viewers can't see what's under the big table at which we sit.

I've often watched this show at home. Lying on my living room sofa, I come up with brilliant responses to Larry's questions about Christianity and how biblical faith relates to today's issues, from abortion to the environment to lifestyle choices.

Yes, at home my imaginary repartee with Larry King is absolutely dazzling.

But this is reality . . . or at any rate, it's live TV. The big camera's red light flashes, and Larry leans forward in his chair, shoulders hunched. He says something like this: "So, Greg Laurie, you're a megachurch pastor. What can you tell us about a Christian response to this issue?"

My mind suddenly goes blank, inoperable. It's a frozen computer screen.

Larry just looks at me and follows up. "Uh, Greg?"

*　*　*

It's a warm night in the South. I can smell the honeysuckle and hear the crickets chirping in the summer darkness. A colleague is driving my wife and me through the streets of a city I've never been to before. We're heading to a meeting of more than 200 pastors who have committed their churches to support one of our evangelistic crusades.

As we pull into the parking lot surrounding the mammoth brick church, I see the usual assortment of minivans with the usual assortment of bumper stickers. "My child is an honor student at Millbrook High." "UNC Tarheels." There are some fish symbols and crosses, too.

But here's what I can't believe: Most of these cars have the same big bumper sticker plastered across the back. All it says, in bright red and black letters, is GREG LAURIE. It feels weird. Embarrassing.

Who in the world is Greg Laurie? I almost think. Then I remember. It's me.

2

TURTLE ON A POST

You may not particularly care who Greg Laurie is. A good deal of the time I don't either. But the question comes to all of us now and then, sometimes in those rare quiet moments, sometimes right in the middle of a busy day.

We wonder, *Who am I, really? Am I the competent professional who looks like he or she has it all together? The scared kid hiding in the dark? The parent, child, pastor, rebel? Am I one—or all—of these roles, and more? And how in the world did I come to this place in my life?*

For me, this "place in my life" is far more deep and wide and wild and good than I ever could have dreamed. I came from broken beginnings . . . my mom's seven broken marriages, broken dishes, lots of broken promises. I hoped that somehow I'd one day have a life that was whole and secure. I wanted to know that I mattered. I dreamed of being significant. I wanted to create things, to make people laugh, to inspire them and touch their lives for good.

When I was a teenager, no one would have thought that any of my dreams could come true. Our family has had some pretty wayward relatives, with a number succumbing to severe alcoholism, and there was no indication that I would be any different.

My older cousin Wayne, a graduate student in the 1960s, was once required to do some psychological testing for a course, so he decided to test me. I was at the peak of my rebellion at the time. Wayne performed the tests and later reported, "There was a lot of anger in Greg and a lot

4

of rebellion, although I don't know if it was pathological or the normal family genes manifesting themselves. But all of us were a bit worried about the way this young man was going."

Not exactly a promising future.

But people's destinies don't have to be determined by their genes or their environment. Your future doesn't have to be dependent on your past. No foregone conclusions. When God breaks into your story, it changes.

For one thing, it gets a lot more interesting.

And though you know how the story will end in the end—literally, happily ever after in heaven—you can't anticipate all the twists and turns along the way. It's like a roller-coaster ride. Sometimes you're in a peaceful place, gently climbing the next hill. Sometimes you're hanging upside down, helpless, pockets spilling quarters. Sometimes you're laughing, screaming, the wind in your hair, on top of the world.

Today, I still can't believe it when I realize that I've been married for 34 years and that Cathe and I have a stable, loving family. No shattered cocktail glasses, no revolving-door relationships. And I haven't been to prison yet, except to visit those inside. No, today—of all things—I'm "Pastor Greg" to a congregation of 15,000 people.

In my old life, it was somewhat of a marvel that I was never expelled from high school, seeing as I spent so much time in the principal's office for mouthing off. Today I'm still verbal. But now I teach about God and the Bible on the radio every day, and I'm told that the audience is about 3 million listeners. I've traveled all over the world preaching the gospel, and I teach on a television program that's aired internationally. I've written about 30 books, as well as thousands of articles and columns.

I don't share this to impress you. If you knew me and who I was and where I came from, you'd simply say, "This is impossible."

And you would be right.

But when God enters your story, it's exhilarating. It's unpredictable and secure at the same time. It can be scary. I would say that it's fun, but that's too light of a word for a pastor to use. So I will say that the journey is full of joy, which is even better.

So why would someone who's written 30 books start another one? Good question.

This book is different from anything I've done before. It's not a set of teachings on particular topics like temptation, marriage, heaven, or faith . . . though it includes all those themes and a whole lot more.

This is a story. It's my story, so, of course, I like it a lot and find it endlessly fascinating. (Just kidding.)

But the reason it's a story worth telling is because a lot of people can relate to it. People like me who weren't the high school quarterback or the cheerleading captain, not the valedictorian or voted "most popular" or "most likely to succeed."

This is a book for people whose sports awards were a set of purple ribbons . . . you know, the ones you get for basically showing up—and sometimes you didn't even do that. This is a story for people who got blue stars that meant something like "adequate" (which really felt more like "inadequate"), rather than those shiny silver stars for "good" or the bold gold stars for "great." It's a story for people who looked out the window and daydreamed of a better life but had no idea how to get there.

I'm writing for people whose lives haven't been great at all, people who come from origins they're ashamed of or who've made choices they regret. I'm here to say that no matter what crazy, broken beginnings you come from, God can change your ending. He changed mine.

Now this doesn't mean that if you're a successful super-achiever you should stop reading! *Everyone* deals with questions about identity, security, significance and destiny.

And whether you came from poverty or privilege, whether you were an underachiever, an overachiever or got lost somewhere in the middle,

God can take hold of your story and change it for good. He uniquely answers the fundamental life questions that beat in every human heart.

In my case, let's just say that when you see a turtle on a fence post, you know he didn't get there by himself. Someone put him there.

And in order to find out just how he arrived at his particular post, the fresh breeze blowing through his hard shell and his little turtle beak smiling in the sunshine, you have to hear his turtle story.

So here's my story.

ONE-NIGHT STAND

In spite of my beginnings, God called me to be an evangelist, of all things. There are just not a whole lot of evangelists out there in the twenty-first-century marketplace. Billy Graham has been the gold standard of that calling in our day; no single person could begin to take his place.

Billy's oldest son, Franklin, is a gifted evangelist like his father. Franklin and I have been close friends for years, and in some ways we are much alike.

But our paths have been very different. Franklin has the blessing of a lifelong relationship with parents who raised him to love God and seek His ways. He's had a mom and dad he could be proud of, parents who've been so proud of him.

I've seen Franklin support his dad and help him walk, just as his dad once helped him walk as a toddler. I've seen Billy give Franklin direct, fatherly advice, and I've seen him tenderly embrace his son with tears.

To be honest, when I've seen their intimate, loving relationship, my heart sometimes constricts with pain and a sense of loss. I love them both . . . but I wish I could have had the experience they share. I've looked with some envy on a son who not only knows who his father *is*, but is also a son and heir whose father is a godly role model—not to mention the greatest evangelist who ever lived.

My story started in quite a different way. I was a bastard, in the technical sense of that ugly term, the illegitimate result of a one-night stand. Some would call me a mistake, my very existence a slip-up that could have been whisked away.

But as I've gotten older, I've seen the impossible happen, in that I can now consider my less-than-honorable beginnings an actual blessing.

Because I grew up in bars with drunks, sleazy skuzzballs and skuzzy sleazeballs, I can relate to people who come from broken beginnings. I know firsthand that God can intervene in damaged lives and restore them. Incredibly, He can make His repairs work backward in time.

Even the hole that I feel when I see friends with their fathers is something God has used for good. I can relate to others who are fatherless. And I've experienced, in a way I otherwise could not have, what it means to rely on God Himself as my heavenly Father.

But I'm getting a little ahead of my story.

To get the whole picture, we have to start with a fiery, gorgeous young woman named Charlene McDaniel.

LOST GIRL

Charlene McDaniel was a country girl raised in a strict, religious home to mind her manners, mop the floors on her hands and knees, and go to church on Sundays. The McDaniels came from the metropolis of Friendship, Arkansas, and when they moved their growing brood to Southern California in the late 1930s, they brought their Southern Baptist values and work ethic with them.

The McDaniels lived two blocks from the Baptist church, and they made sure that their nine children were there every time the doors were open. When the kids weren't at church or school, they were expected to be at home, tending the bountiful gardens where Charles McDaniel raised millions of vegetables every summer. There were also rabbits, pigs and chickens to feed, a cow to milk and rooms to clean.

The McDaniel home was a secure, ordered environment. Charles worked as a foreman at a chemical plant. When World War II began, his wife, Stella, took a job at what had been a swimsuit factory but was turned by the war effort into a parachute plant. Both Charles and Stella were generous and hospitable; all the kids knew that on Sundays they could each invite a friend home for Sunday dinner. This meant at least 20 people were gathered around the McDaniels' big dining room table with its snowy tablecloth and shining white plates. They ate well: Sunday dinner was always fried chicken and a beef roast, green beans with mashed potatoes, fried corn off the cob, fried okra, ripe red sliced tomatoes, and steaming, tender biscuits with fresh berry jam and homemade butter.

If the McDaniels' hospitality was open and welcoming, their family rules were strict and tight. The children were to be temperate, compliant and obedient. They were not to play cards, dance, go swimming with members of the opposite sex, or engage in any other "worldly" activities that might tempt them down the disorderly road to hell.

Charlene McDaniel was many things, but she was never temperate, compliant or obedient. She had "rebel" written all over her DNA. Needless to say, she chafed under the tight structure of her parents' home.

One evening when she was about 16, Charlene did the unthinkable. Wearing pants—an unacceptable behavior in the McDaniel home—she went to a youth group activity with kids from a Baptist church that was more liberal than her parents' church.

When she arrived home that evening, her father strode into the living room. A well-constructed fire was burning in the fireplace, and Charles carefully laid a large pair of sewing shears on the mantel.

"Charlene," he said quietly. "Go take those pants off."

Charlene left the room for a few minutes and returned wearing a nice, modest skirt, the pants in her hand. Peeking through the French doors that separated the living room from the dining room, the younger kids watched as their father took the heavy shears, hacked the pants into pieces and threw them into the fire.

Charlene said nothing. She simply turned and left the room, her blue eyes smoldering.

It was no big surprise about a year later when she left for good.

During the war, the streets of nearby Long Beach were thick with sailors. When the fleet was in, many young enlisted men showed up at the local Baptist churches, and the McDaniels, with their gift of hospitality, hosted many of them for meals.

One Saturday evening, Charlene got her younger sister Willie to help her with a secret mission. Willie watched as Charlene packed a hard-sided suitcase with a few sets of clothes, underwear, a hairbrush and toiletries. Willie carried the small case to the Baptist church and carefully pushed it under a narrow outdoor wall opening that was designed for plumbing access.

On Sunday morning, the McDaniels were lined up in their pew, their ribbons starched and their pants precisely pressed, singing Baptist hymns . . . and at some point during the service, Charlene slipped out, retrieved her suitcase, met up with a sailor named Ken and ran away to marry him. She was 17.

Theirs was not one of the great love matches of all time. Charlene had learned that she had two tremendous assets: She was not only beautiful; she was one of those young women who exude seductive power. Later she was often compared with Marilyn Monroe, and for good reason. Men found her irresistible, and she used that allure to her own ends.

Ken was her means of escape from her parents' home. She stayed with him for a few years, had a baby named Doug, and then left Ken for another man. With that husband, she gave birth to a stillborn child. Grieving and restless, she wanted out.

Evidently she still had a fair degree of persuasive power over her younger sister Willie, because she got Willie—now an experienced escape artist's assistant—to help her leave that second husband so that Charlene could engage, full-force, in a party lifestyle. The bright lights and shiny lifestyle of Hollywood beckoned . . . but if she couldn't have that, she'd settle for dark bars and a parade of flashy men who talked big but lived small.

It was 1952. Queen Elizabeth ascended to the throne of England. U.S. President Harry Truman was preparing to engage North Korea and China in peace negotiations. *The Today Show*, *The Adventures of Ozzie and Harriet* and *American Bandstand* debuted on television. *Singing in the Rain* and *High Noon* played on the big screen. Nat King Cole was at the top of the music charts.

Long Beach, California, was still filled with sailors; Charlene had no trouble attracting them. She'd sit in bars at night, a vision with platinum blond hair, flawless skin, crystal eyes and shapely figure. She'd ask a man to light her cigarette, lock him with her gaze . . . and it was all over.

Somewhere along the line, she met a particular sailor. He was a limber strawberry blond-haired guy who swirled her around the dance floor and made her laugh. I don't know anything further—perhaps their connection was no more than a one-night stand.

Eventually, after the sailor was long gone from her picture, Charlene discovered she was pregnant.

Never one to lack for options, she quickly married a guy named Kim. And by the time December 10, 1952, arrived and she gave birth to a son, no one was asking a whole lot of questions as to just who the baby's father was.

She named me Gregory Mitchell.

The last name on my birth certificate was that of her husband Kim, but as I began to grow up, he sure didn't feel like a dad.

My Aunt Willie remembers an occasion when I was just a young toddler, sitting in a wooden highchair, my chubby legs and bare feet dangling, while my mom spooned cereal into my mouth. Kim, probably drunk, decided that I was not eating fast enough. He grabbed a thick wooden ruler and started hitting me, over and over, on the soles of my soft little baby feet.

I don't remember that particular event. But I do remember the ongoing blows to my small soul as the years rolled on and our family slipped further and further into the chaos of alcoholism.

5

POGO

A thousand years ago, when I was young, an opossum named "Pogo" starred in one of the most popular comic strips of the day. Pogo was quick, funny and mischievous. He was always getting into trouble.

My Aunt Willie, who evidently decided to resign from her unofficial job of helping my mother escape from constraints, decided that I was just like Pogo. Like many kids who have a vivid imagination and spend a lot of time alone, I escaped from realities I did not like by drawing, pulling pranks and making people laugh. So I became "Pogo" to my family.

Some of the realities I didn't like were hard to avoid. I remember when I was just a little guy, sitting on the floor in my pajamas on Christmas night. The colored lights on the artificial tree blinked on and off, and the tinsel shimmered whenever a breeze blew through the open window.

But then I looked at my mom, and there she was, passed out drunk on the sofa. I didn't really know any other reality than the life we lived, but I remember thinking, *This is not how it is supposed to be.*

So much for Christmas.

My mom would often leave me alone while she went out. I'd fall asleep at first, but then I'd wake up, huddled in my bed, and wait for her. I wanted her to come home . . . but I *didn't* want her to come home, because every night was the same: I'd hear the door open and breathe a sigh of relief. Then I'd hear the tinkle of ice and drinks being poured, then the shouting and crash of things thrown against walls. Sometimes the neighbors would call or the police would come, but most often it would all end, eventually, and it would be very quiet. I'd get up and my mom and whoever she was with would be passed out, maybe on the floor, or maybe in a naked tangle on the bed.

I saw things no child should see.

Sometimes my mom would come home alone, and while that was a relief, it was still stressful. She was always drunk. She'd call someone and yell into the phone, or she'd yell for me.

"Pogo!" she'd shout. "Wake up and make me a fried-egg sandwich!"

I'd get up, fry an egg and slip it between pieces of buttered toast. Usually she'd thank me, eat it and fall asleep. One night she threw it at me, along with the plate it was served on. It barely missed my head before it crashed against the wall.

Whether she thanked me or cursed me, it was all the same to her: The next morning she never remembered anything from the night before. If I tried to bring things up that had happened, she never wanted to talk about it.

I didn't hold it against her. It was like she was two people: sober mom, drunken mom. I learned to deal with each of them differently.

But I also learned not to trust drunks. I'm not sure I trusted anyone. I walled off my emotions so that I wouldn't hurt, and I lowered my expectations of people so that I wouldn't be disappointed.

Still, I could be gullible. One night a guy came home with my mom. He was an animator at Disney. I couldn't believe it! All I wanted was to be a cartoonist when I grew up. Walt Disney was one of my heroes.

The guy could see that I didn't quite believe he really worked with Disney. He took a pencil and drew an absolutely perfect Mickey Mouse on a sheet of white paper. I stared at it, my mouth open.

"Now," he said, smiling, "all you have to do is take this same pencil, put it under your pillow tonight, and when you wake up in the morning, you'll be able to draw Mickey Mouse just like me!"

I believed in magic, or at least I wanted to. I took the paper and pencil and went to bed. I couldn't wait for the morning.

But when I woke up and carefully pulled the pencil from underneath my pillow, I discovered that I couldn't draw Mickey Mouse any better than I could the night before. I realized the guy had lied. He just wanted to get rid of me so that he could be alone with my mom. And I realized that I shouldn't believe in magic—for *me*, at least—after all.

6

MR. NOBODY

As my mother continued her serial marriages, racking up rocky relationships and rolling on, it wasn't always convenient to have a little boy as part of her package. My older half-brother Doug lived with his father most of the time, but he also spent time with our grandparents, and occasionally I did, too.

I remember a picture of Jesus on their living room wall. He was tan, His lank blondish hair parted in the middle. He was looking somewhere else, not at me. He didn't seem like He had any connection to my life, and I was more interested in playing with my plastic army men on the planked wooden floor.

I'd line them up and have them ambush each other. I'd melt the losers on the big floor heater that warmed the living room during the winter. The little soldiers would get soft, and then their arms and legs would bend, and then they'd gradually lose their shape and slide down into a warm puddle of plastic goo.

Sometimes in the evenings my grandparents would sit in their matching La-Z-Boy chairs while I lay on the floor. They'd take hunks of Mama Stella's coarse, salty cornbread, crumble it into tall glasses of cold buttermilk, and eat it with a spoon. We'd watch *Gunsmoke* and *Bonanza* on the big old black-and-white television with the rabbit-ear antennae on top.

Mama Stella and Daddy Charles loved Billy Graham crusades, and we'd watch those, too. Actually, Billy Graham reminded me a little bit of Marshal Dillon on *Gunsmoke*; he was strong and good. But he was as remote as that Jesus looking the other way, up on my grandparents' living room wall.

Every day or so, the Helms' bakery truck would pull into Mama Stella's driveway. It was an old-fashioned panel truck custom-fitted with massive wooden drawers. The Helms man would hop out, unbolt the back doors and pull open a drawer full of hot doughnuts and freshly baked pastries.

Mama Stella would buy glazed doughnuts, crisp them in a hot oven, and melt sweet cream butter on top. They must have had about a thousand calories apiece, but Mama Stella wasn't one to scrimp on calories.

She did scrimp on affection, however. Her reticence had more to do with how *she* was raised than how she felt about me, but back then I didn't know that. She occasionally squeezed my shoulders, but Mama Stella primarily expressed love through food and hospitality, not through hugs and affirmation. As a small boy I loved the food . . . but I missed the hugs.

My grandfather could be harsh. If I broke the rules, he'd use a switch or a leather belt to teach me a lesson. I screamed and cried, but it never stopped him. Oddly enough, I didn't resent him for it. The pain showed me that there were parameters in life to live by—something I would forget about later.

By placing me with my grandparents, my mom put me in the very life she had run away from. I got a taste of what she had experienced. Though I didn't understand it then, maybe I sensed, down deep, why she was on a perpetual quest for love.

For my part, I was comforted during those contradictory days of hot doughnuts and cold relationships by an unseen friend who was always with me.

If this was a nice Christian book, here's where I would say that I first sensed Jesus, even though I didn't yet know Him. But I have to tell you, though I know *now* that God was with me throughout those lonely days of my childhood, I didn't know it then.

No, back then my unseen companion was an imaginary friend I named "Mr. Nobody."

At night I would lie in my little bed. The sheets were fresh and starched, but the room was bare. No toys on shelves, no posters on the walls. It looked like a room at a boarding house, which fit, because I felt like a tenant.

I'd pull the clean white sheet and the cotton coverlet over my head, and I'd shine my little flashlight to make a warm glow. And then I'd talk to Mr. Nobody.

He was very accommodating. He always listened.

Now, before you start worrying about my mental state, let's remember that it's not unusual for small children to have imaginary friends. Experts say that two-thirds of kids do so, and Yale psychologists have found that imaginative children who create fantasy companions actually tend to have well-adjusted and creative adult years.[1]

I don't know that my wife would agree with that. But the point is that loneliness sharpened an already acute longing in me for warmth, connection and tenderness. So I compensated by connecting with my imaginary buddy (though because I named him "Mr. Nobody," it's obvious that I was quite clear about his actual status).

But the McDaniels' home was a stable one. There was no screaming, fighting or drinking. We went to bed early and woke up with the sun. I was relieved to be free from the madness of life with my mom . . . but I missed her, and I worried about her. I felt it was my job to protect her, as though I was the parent and she was the child.

I would go home and live with her for a while, and then she'd send me somewhere else.

Note

1. Angela Parisi, "Imaginary Companions Can Be Child's Fast Friends," for *HealthDay* online, December 13, 2007. http://news.healingwell.com/index.php?p=news1&id=522821 (accessed January 2008).

7

KEEP YOUR HEAD UP

When I was six, and then again when I was ten, my mother sent me off to military school. I don't know why she expected that I, with my inherited rebel DNA, would do well in a military environment, but maybe my "doing well" was beside the point.

Off I went.

The school, Southern California Military Academy, was in Long Beach, though it no longer exists. My memories of it are hazy, but it would have served as a great setting for a movie.

In fact, long after my time there, the school's uniforms, its motto and many of its students were used in a forgettable Sylvester Stallone film called *Over the Top*.

I remember the school as drab and gray with squared corners. I was only six years old when I went there the first time, and I lived in a barracks that I recall now as something like a World War II movie.

I felt like I was in prison. We slept on hard, narrow bunks, and every morning we stood at attention in our quarters while our uniforms, possessions, shoes and hair all went through inspection. I remember someone giving me the tip that I could use a woman's nylon stocking to shine my little shoes.

The commandant of our small camp was called "The General." He was actually missing an arm due to a combat wound, and wore his uniform pinned up at the sleeve. We saluted him very carefully. Students who used inappropriate language had their mouths washed out with soap. Those who committed more serious offenses were whaled with a wooden cheese paddle (a paddle with holes in it).

Some kids went AWOL—they hopped the fence and ran away. I never did. I didn't know where to go.

In my blurred memories of the time, I do remember one thing quite clearly. In my head were the words of a Rogers and Hammerstein song from the musical *Carousel*. We sang it many times in our mandatory chapel services, and the lyrics about walking through the wind with hope in your heart struck a chord within me. I would sing them over and over to myself, and I felt that I wasn't alone, even though the gray storms of military school were daunting.

The strict school did have its positives. When I returned there as an older kid, I did better academically than I had in a less-disciplined environment. When I had someone standing over me—particularly if that individual was a one-armed commandant wielding a cheese paddle—I studied more and talked less. I earned *As* and *Bs*, as opposed to the lower grades I got in public school, where I'd daydream and stare out the classroom window . . . no doubt chatting with Mr. Nobody.

As a little boy at military school, I missed my mom. One weekend when she wanted me to come and see her at home, I was overjoyed. But instead of driving the 22 miles to pick me up, she arranged to have me come to her by bus.

I remember sitting alone on a sticky wooden bench in the Long Beach bus station, wearing my uniform. I had my little duffel bag with me, and I held it in my lap. I could smell old cigarettes, and I clutched my bag closer when big men passed by my bench and looked me over.

Finally the bus came. I climbed on and perched on a seat near the driver. But I wasn't sure which stop to get off on, so I rode to San Clemente instead of getting off in Newport Beach. I had a dime, and I called my mom from a pay phone at the bus station. As I recall, she had been having a party with her friends. She said she'd been very worried about me. She sent someone else to pick me up.

Looking back in time, I'm horrified at what could have happened. I could have been abducted, or worse. Little boys traveling alone don't tend to fare well in dimly lit public bus stations.

One day a special parade was held at Southern California Military Academy. This was when the television series *Lassie* was at the height of its fame. (For young readers or those from Mars, *Lassie* featured a valiant, courageous collie who constantly rescued her young master, Timmy, from all kinds of dangers, toils and snares.)

Timmy and Lassie came to my school. I remember standing at the edge of the parade grounds, no doubt at attention, watching Timmy at the head of a parade of marching students, waving, his other arm on his enormous, fluffy golden and white dog, who strode with him in perfect time.

Lassie wagged her tail, her bright eyes shining with adoration whenever she looked at him . . . and I thought that I would have given anything to be Timmy.

My military experience came to a welcome close when I returned home to live with my mother. By now she had married and divorced again. But then something happened that was an absolute surprise, and I experienced the closest thing I ever would to a wholesome, Timmy-and-Lassie life.

8

NEW NAME

My mom met a man named Oscar Laurie. Oscar didn't smoke cigarettes or drink to excess, and he wasn't a flashy barfly. He was an attorney, a well-read man with a moral lifestyle. He married my mother, and we moved to his home in New Jersey. We lived together in a spacious apartment with thick white carpeting. There was a doorman at the entrance to our building. I'd never seen anything like it.

I'd never seen leaves falling from trees in the autumn. I was thrilled by the snow. And I was amazed when my mother's new husband didn't see me as just a pesky kid to send away.

Instead, Oscar Laurie formally adopted me and gave me his name.

Oscar also gave me boundaries. He corrected my language and admonished me to do well in school. He even took me to the local jail to show me where I would end up if I made the wrong decisions in life.

I had my mother's DNA, of course, so part of me rebelled at all the rules and structure. The other part of me loved it. I began to uncoil a little, like a person whose fist has been clenched for so long that it takes a while for the hand to open and relax.

Christmas was different now. Oscar bought me an incredible racecar track with two little cars that whizzed around with working headlights. He patiently built it with me, and then got down on the floor as we raced the cars together by the light of the shimmering Christmas tree.

It was easy for me to call Oscar "Dad." I trusted him.

When I was still small he gave me a big, new bike. A two-wheeler. I felt like a big guy riding it, even as I was reassured by the training wheels that stabilized it so that I wouldn't fall off.

One day Oscar decided it was time for me to learn to ride it on my own. He unbolted the training wheels.

He set the bike upright, held it straight and told me to climb aboard.

I was unsure, unsteady and unwilling, but Oscar's calm voice reassured me. "I will be right behind you, son!"

I grabbed the handlebars with a death grip.

"Okay," said Oscar. "Here we go!"

He pushed the bike forward.

"Are you there?" I cried.

"I'm right here," Oscar said. "You're doing fine!"

The bike was going faster now. I was pedaling, my dad was pushing, my hair was blowing.

"Are you there, Dad?" I yelled again.

"I'm right here, Greg," Oscar replied.

Faster still. I was grinning and yelling, balanced, and I'd forgotten about my fear. The only problem was that my poor dad was having to run so fast to steady me while I had all the fun.

"You okay, Dad?" I yelled.

Silence.

"Dad, are you *there?!*"

I turned to look for him and he was way behind me, smiling a huge smile. He'd let go to show me I could do it on my own . . . and I had, until I'd realized he wasn't there.

I lost my balance and crashed in a heap, crying.

Oscar came running. He scooped me up and held me close. "You're doing great, Greg!" he whispered. "And I'm right here for you."

When they got engaged, Oscar had given my mom a four-carat diamond ring. It flashed on her slender hand like silver fire. My mom had always been attracted to big rings and bright lights, but this was the real thing. And so was Oscar.

But one day she went to the beach and lost her brilliant ring in the sand. "Oh, well," she told Oscar. "It was beautiful while it lasted."

I should have known that the same thing would happen with Oscar.

A few years went by. One day when I came out after the final bell at school, there was my mother. She was sitting at the wheel of her big black Cadillac, her platinum hair shining in the afternoon sun.

"Get in," she said.

The car was full of boxes and suitcases, so maybe we were off to a new adventure.

"What's going on?" I said.

"We're going to Hawaii," she said.

My eyebrows went up. *Hawaii!* It sounded so luxurious and tropical; I could see the palm trees dancing in the breeze and hear the distant crash of the surf. New Jersey was nothing by comparison.

"Great!" I said, smiling. "Where's Dad?"

She didn't smile back.

"He's not coming."

9

TROUBLE IN PARADISE

My mother had met some other man. And here we were, leaving the only father I'd ever known, to fly off to Honolulu.

I was in shock. But I was a kid, easily distractible. When we got off the plane, the first thing that touched me was the fragrant, balmy air, warm on my skin. My feet were itching to escape my New Jersey shoes. Hawaii felt like freedom.

There was a man waiting to meet us. I'll call him Eddie. He was the opposite of Oscar Laurie. Where Oscar was a smaller man with conservative buttoned-down East Coast style, Eddie was big, well over six feet. His hair was dark and oily, his shirts open, his style carefree. He looked like a poor man's Dean Martin, and acted like a Rat Pack wannabe.

I don't even know how Eddie and my mom had met. But now here she was for him, a gorgeous woman at the peak of her beauty, a trophy wife before the phrase was even coined.

The only problem was that she came with some baggage. Not just the suitcases, but also a young boy. A little boy who now missed the only father he had ever known.

When we arrived at Eddie's house, I was impressed. It was wide and expansive, decorated in early '60s Hawaii style. There was a lot of dark wood furniture, mod lamps, avocado green fabrics and large glass sliding doors to a massive back yard with a huge swimming pool.

Then we came to my bedroom. It was almost an exact reproduction of the room I had so abruptly left in New Jersey. I saw the same bedspread, the same stuffed animals, the same toys. There were also a few new things, like a little electronic picture of a lake with a boy peeing into it. The height of '60s hi-tech, it changed color from blue to yellow.

I grinned. It was naughty.

Oscar would never have approved.

Eddie was my mom's usual kind of guy. He lived in the moment. He just wanted to have fun. Where Oscar had been proper, controlled and trustworthy, Eddie was crass, shifty and had an explosive temper. Oscar drank only occasionally; Eddie was a certified drunk. As an attorney, Oscar was a member of the New Jersey Bar Association. Eddie was a member of the bar culture. He owned a tavern and was chief operator, bartender and bouncer, all in one.

Eddie was also trying to escape from his past. He eventually told me how he was in combat during World War II, and while he was trying to escape from his tank, which was on fire, an enemy grenade had exploded. He'd taken shrapnel in his leg and had suffered near-constant pain ever since.

Looking back, I can see how Eddie must have used alcohol to dull the pain. When he was sober—which wasn't very often—he could be fairly pleasant. But when he had had a few drinks, he became a mean, violent drunk.

Something in me snapped at this point. During my time in military school I had tried to be a good boy. In the moves since, I'd dutifully tried to adapt to the changing worlds my mother created with multiple husbands, new schools and new homes. I'd tried to convince myself it was normal.

Sometimes I'd even reassured myself that my life was better than those of people at school who had both parents at home and had to live by curfews, do their homework and eat their vegetables. After all, I was free to come and go as I pleased. I could go to school barefoot.

I was living the carefree life, the life without rules, the life that some of my friends envied. I had a tricked-out room and lots of stuff. I even had my little ink-black poodle, Nikki, who had made the trek from New Jersey, gone through a long quarantine and now was by my side. She wasn't Lassie and I wasn't Timmy, but she loved me.

But I decided there was no reason to keep trying to be a good boy. I might as well try to take advantage of this situation with Eddie. He always seemed to have plenty of cash on hand. So I tried a test, something I would have never attempted with Oscar. One day I came to him while he was sprawled in his easy chair, watching TV.

"Hey, Diddly," I said. ("Diddly" was the ridiculous name that my mom had decided I should call him. I didn't care. All I knew is that I sure wasn't going to call him—or anyone else except Oscar Laurie—"Dad.")

"Uh," said Eddie.

"Can I have $5?"

In the '60s, for me, $5 was a huge sum. My allowance with Oscar had been 50 cents a week, and I had to work hard for it. Now I was asking this lout for 10 times that.

"Sure," Eddie muttered.

He reached in his back pocket, pulled out a crisp $5 bill, and extended it toward me. He never even made eye contact. The exchange meant nothing to him. It didn't mean anything to me, either.

But I did have $5, and now I knew how to endure life with Eddie.

UNDER THE SEA

Eddie's bar, which I'll call The Lava Lounge, was beneath an oceanfront hotel on Waikiki, the world's most famous beach. You took a few steps down, away from the sunny sand and the balmy breeze, into a pseudo-nautical world that smelled like smoke, booze and mildew. There was a built-in saltwater fish tank, with seahorses bobbing around in it, and lots of fishing nets strung up on the old wood walls. Hanging from the dark brown ceiling were puffer-fish. They'd been shellacked to keep them in their unfortunate and inflated state. Some had little lights inside; these threw a dim, golden light in the dark room.

The bar was draped with fishing lines and big hemp ropes. It faced a big, thick-glass window that gave patrons a shadowed, underwater view of the hotel swimming pool.

Whenever I was in the pool, I'd take a deep breath and swim down to the bottom. I'd press my face against the thick glass separating the swimming pool from the bar, and make faces at the glassy-eyed patrons sitting there. They looked at first like they'd been shellacked like the puffer fish, but then they'd smile and wave, and I always got a charge out of that. It was pretty easy to make drunk people laugh.

Sometimes my mom would hold a cocktail napkin up to the pool window. I'd dive down to see that she'd scrawled "LUNCH!" on it. I'd surface, towel off and have my usual: a hamburger, French fries and a vanilla malt at the bar.

I made friends with the characters who made the bar their home. Call it a survival skill, but if I didn't connect with the adults in my mother's world, I would have spent a lot of time alone.

I did have some friends outside. The local adult "beach boys" charged tourists to take them out on the outriggers for rides. Some of them were pure-blooded Hawaiian. One who went by the name of Steamboat became a friend. He taught me how to make straw hats, Hawaiian style, and took me on free rides in his outrigger. We'd laugh while exhausted tourists did all the paddling, sweating through their genuine island experience. I felt like a local.

But, as the cliché goes, there was trouble in paradise.

One evening Eddie and my mom and I were eating a late dinner on the patio of our beautiful home in the hills of Honolulu. As I was taking a bite, the fork scraped against my two front teeth. They protruded a bit; I had a chipmunk look at that stage.

Eddie banged his fist on the table, and the plates rattled.

"Stop scraping that fork on your teeth!" he shouted.

I knew not to rile him further. I nodded and waited a while before I tried to take another bite.

But I was hungry . . . and my next bite sent Eddie through the roof.

"I told you to stop it!" he exploded. "And I meant *stop it!*" He shook and cursed and screamed at me; my teeth scraping had sent him completely out of control.

After that night, I began to be genuinely afraid of him. But I was more afraid for my mother. She was feisty even when she wasn't drinking, and alcohol made her even wilder. Eddie was a huge guy, but when they fought she thought nothing of hurling heavy ashtrays or a lamp at him or calling him names.

Some mornings I'd go out to the living room after they'd had a night of it and there would be broken glass, shelves torn down, lamps with their cords ripped out of the electrical sockets. One night they took out a whole plate glass window.

The only safe place for me at night was in my New Jersey-cloned bedroom. I'd hug my little dog Nikki close and talk to her. She was just like Mr. Nobody, I guess, except that she had the virtue of being real and she could wag her tail and lick my face. She was a reminder of Oscar—he had given her to me. I loved her.

One night, very late, after a lot of drinking, partying and arguing, I was suddenly woken up. My mother was shaking my shoulder. There were tears in her eyes, and her words were slurred.

"Mickey has been hit by a car!"

I thought she meant her close friend in California, Mickey, who was like an aunt to me.

"Oh, no!" I said. "How is she doing? Are you going to go to California to see her?"

"Didn't you hear me?" my mom raged. "I didn't say 'Mickey!' I said 'Nikki!' "

I couldn't believe it. My little furry dog was all I really cared about. And now she was gone.

On one of his good days, Eddie went out and bought a little black poodle that looked just like Nikki. (Eddie really was into facsimiles.) We named the replacement dog "Pogo."

On his bad days, Eddie beat the dog. When he was drunk and unsteady he'd hit Pogo, and that defiant little dog would bite him in the hand, drawing blood.

Eddie would hit again, and Pogo would bite again.

I liked it when Pogo fought back.

But most of the time, the violence wasn't funny. It was terrifying, and it came to a head the night that Eddie nearly beat my mother to death with a heavy wooden statue.

She lay limp on the floor in a spreading pool of blood. Eddie screamed at me to go back to bed. I edged back toward my room, eased the door shut and climbed out the window. I ran to the neighbors. They called the police.

And in the end, we left Eddie for good, trading the chaos of Waikiki for a supposedly brand-new life back in California.

But by now the 1960s were in full swing. And for the hippies, surfers and acid heads of Southern California, that meant sex, drugs and rock 'n' roll.

BLOWIN' IN THE WIND

When I close my eyes and think back to the day our Boeing 707 touched down on the runway at Los Angeles International Airport, the hot tarmac shimmering in the haze, I remember my mom sitting with her cheek propped on one hand, staring out the airplane window—and I wonder what she wondered about her future. Her Marilyn Monroe hair and sparkly earrings were as beautiful as ever . . . but by that point, Marilyn Monroe was long gone, dead by suicide in 1962.

The 1960s was a wild decade to grow up in. The glamour of the 1950s world of big hair, big bands and big American dreams had passed, taken down when President Kennedy was assassinated in 1963 and the curtain came down on Camelot. The cookie-cutter conformity of the '50s was gone as well. Many people had decided the conventional American dream wasn't for them; they wanted a new culture, new music, a new age they called Aquarius.

New visions of mushroom clouds lurked on the horizon. The Cold War threat was somehow more sinister than the old-fashioned wars of the past. Schoolchildren routinely practiced bomb drills in their classrooms, as if diving under your little wooden desk could save you from The Big One.

Meanwhile more and more American troops were fighting in the jungles of Vietnam, sweating and dying. Protestors were hitting the streets of America, screaming obscenities at Establishment icons.

You could feel the contradictions in the music, poetry and dress of the day. On one hand there was an almost innocent delight in color, texture, love, freedom and flowers, but the hippies' happy tapestry was woven also with darker threads of defiance. Many middle-aged Americans were mystified: What had happened to the perky, positive outlook that had kicked off the decade?

By mid-1967, *Time* magazine stepped up to analyze the times that had changed with a psychedelic cover story titled "The Hippies: Philosophy of a Subculture." "Hippies preach altruism and mysticism, honesty, joy and nonviolence," *Time* reporters observed, in a tone that sounds naïve today. But reporters also pointed to a certain unreality among hippies, "a cult whose mystique derives essentially from the influence of hallucinogenic drugs."[1]

Ah, yes. The drugs.

January 1967 unleashed this new wave of hippiedom with the "Human Be-In" in San Francisco's Golden Gate Park. About 30,000 kids gathered for 12 hours of counter-cultural solidarity. If you had traipsed through their ranks, the smell of marijuana would have been thick in the air. You'd have talked with the brown-eyed girl with a daisy behind her ear or the thin shirtless boy smoking a joint, and they would have told you that they reject the status quo of their parents' generation. They were against middle-class morality and the burgeoning war in Vietnam. They were for communal living, higher consciousness, free love and peace.

(Just in case the peace part didn't work out, security for the Be-In was provided by the Hell's Angels motorcycle gang.)

The former Harvard professor and psychedelic-drug enthusiast Dr. Timothy Leary exhorted the crowd to "turn on, tune in, drop out," though I doubt anyone attending really needed much encouragement to do any of those things. Bands like Jefferson Airplane, the Grateful Dead and Quicksilver Messenger Service played, and an "underground chemist" provided White Lightning LSD that had been custom-made for the event.

Later that spring, the song "San Francisco (Be Sure to Wear Flowers in Your Hair)" hit the charts. Kids at love-ins swayed to its gentle rhythms as flowers sprouted in the air right before them, courtesy of the acid dancing in their brains.

As the Beatles put it, everybody was getting high, with a little help from their friends.

I remember when the Beatles first came from England to America and played on *The Ed Sullivan Show*. I saw it at my grandparents' house. It was 1964. Mama Stella and Daddy Charles sat in their matching La-Z-Boy chairs, shocked by these mop-haired boys playing a new kind of music. They were like millions of bewildered older people across America, asking themselves, *What is it about the Beatles that makes teenaged girls scream and swoon?*

An estimated 73 million people were watching their big old boxy televisions that night in 1964. Before the TV cameras started rolling, 23-year-old John Lennon was so nervous that he taped his song lyrics to the back of his guitar.

These boys from Liverpool wore *ties* on *The Ed Sullivan Show*. If you watch the black-and-white archival footage today, the Beatles look like four clean-cut Mormons, so it's hard to believe what a scandal they were to middle-class America. But parents who were used to Pat Boone were sure that the Beatles were out to sabotage their teenagers' morals.

The superstar status that followed their Ed Sullivan gig—Beatlemania—led John Lennon to make his infamous claim, "Christianity will go. It will vanish and shrink. . . . We're more popular than Jesus now; I don't know which will go first, rock 'n' roll or Christianity. Jesus was all right but his disciples were thick and ordinary. It's them twisting it that ruins it for me."[2]

After Lennon's comment, many radio stations in the U.S. banned the Beatles. Life on the road became even wilder for the band, with death threats as well as the usual groupies, crazies and hangers-on. In 1966 they decided to stop touring.

By 1967, the Beatles' little skinny ties were long gone. That summer they released *Sgt. Pepper's Lonely Hearts Club Band.* I can still see that album cover in my head, with the Beatles' Day-Glo silk pseudo-military uniforms, gold-braided epaulets and drooping moustaches.

Behind the Fab Four on the album were a crowd of icons, everyone from Albert Einstein to Karl Marx, from Mae West to W. C. Fields, from Shirley Temple to Lawrence of Arabia. Lennon, McCartney, Harrison and Starr stand next to wax-works replicas of themselves as they appeared in the early '60s. They're looking down on the word "Beatles" spelled out in flowers, like a grave. Farewell to the innocent past.

In June 1967, the Monterey Pop Festival brought together The Byrds, Jefferson Airplane, The Who, Buffalo Springfield, The Grateful Dead, The Mamas and the Papas, Indian sitar player Ravi Shankar, Otis Redding, Janis Joplin and Jimi Hendrix—who decisively ended his set by smashing his guitar and setting it on fire.

In July, the Doors' single "Light My Fire" hit No. 1 on the charts. Drug-fueled lead singer Jim Morrison fused rock, poetry and sex into a psychedelic experience that captured the spirit of the age. When the band appeared on *The Ed Sullivan Show*, they were asked to change the lyrics so that they weren't quite so suggestive. No surprise that when the live cameras rolled, Jim Morrison "forgot" to do so and went on to wallow in fiery sex imagery that scandalized censors and older viewers alike. But I remember walking on Corona del Mar beach one sunny summer day when it seemed like every single transistor radio there was blaring "Light My Fire."

By autumn of '67, the fresh flowers of the "Summer of Love" had faded in an ugly fall. In San Francisco's Haight-Ashbury district, center

BLOWIN' IN THE WIND

of the hippie scene, the idealism of the early days had disintegrated into crime, hunger, overdoses, junkies and dirty needles. The neighborhood had gone commercial: Middle-aged tourists came in buses with Kodak cameras around their necks to gawk at the flower children and take their pictures. The infamous Psychedelic Shop on Haight Street closed in protest; its owners moved back to the Midwest. Young people were sleeping in the streets.

Beatle George Harrison was disappointed when he came to visit the San Francisco scene. "I expected them to be nice and clean and happy," he remarked. But the hippies weren't the beautiful people he had in mind. Instead, said George, they were "hideous, spotty little teenagers."[3]

A well-known neighborhood acid dealer named Shob was found stabbed to death, his right arm severed just above the elbow. Police stopped another drug dealer and found the bloody arm behind the seat of his van. Crime was up. Summer hippies had gone back to school. Winter was coming.

On October 7, the Haight's hardcore flower children held a mock funeral procession, proclaiming the death of the hippie. Pallbearers carried a wooden coffin draped in black. It was filled with psychedelic posters, bongs and beads. The Summer of Love had passed away.

The ungentle years that followed convulsed America. Martin Luther King, Jr.'s powerful voice of nonviolent social change was stilled by an assassin's bullet. Rioting erupted in city centers across the U.S. Bobby Kennedy, one of the few politicians young people felt they could connect with, was gunned down in Los Angeles during his campaign for the presidency. Body bags continued coming home from Vietnam. The Black Panthers, the Weathermen and other groups promoted violence as a means to social change. Though the horrors of Kent State were still in the future, hippies fought with policemen on the streets; college campuses seethed with unrest.

Many of the hippies who had left Haight-Ashbury made their way to a simpler country lifestyle in communes like Hog Farm outside Los Angeles. One group, "The Family," settled in at Spahn Ranch, a broken-down farm and movie set. They were led by Charles Manson, a mesmerizing Rasputin-like ex-convict who had spent 17 of his 32 years in prison.

One evening in August 1969—the week before the Woodstock Festival in New York celebrated peace, love and a new age dawning—members of the Manson Family crept into the secluded home of a Hollywood acquaintance and savagely murdered five people, stabbing them again and again and again. Actress Sharon Tate was found covered in blood, her nearly full-term unborn baby butchered as well.

The next night, the Manson Family descended on a middle-aged couple in an exclusive L.A. suburb. They stabbed them hundreds of times, and left a fork sticking out of the husband's abdomen and a misspelled message on the refrigerator door scrawled in the victims' blood: *Healter Skelter.*

Fear and loathing gripped people all over the country. Later that fall, when Charles Manson was finally arrested, he told police over and over, "I'm only a mirror."[4] Most of Manson's narcissistic, hate-filled diatribes made no sense, but people couldn't help but wonder about the values of the hippie movement Manson had said he was reflecting. Maybe peace and love were just pipe dreams; maybe there was a dark side no one had counted on.

In December 1969, Livermore, California, hosted the infamous Altamont Speedway Free Festival. It was supposed to be a West Coast Woodstock, full of music, drugs and happy naked people. But the Hell's Angels, paid in beer to provide security, didn't get the peace and love memo. Using lead-weighted pool cues, they beat up stoned attendees. While a red-caped Mick Jagger was singing The Rolling Stones' signature song, "Sympathy for the Devil," gang members knifed a young man to death, just yards from the stage. Movie crews filming the Stones' documentary *Gimme Shelter* caught the murder on camera.

Soon, some of the most flamboyant icons of the '60s met their ends as well. Janis Joplin, so hot and primeval in life, was found cold and stiff on a hotel room floor, a pack of cigarettes in one hand, $4.50 in the other, bad heroin in her veins. Jim Morrison was dead in the bathtub, cold foam on his lips and narcotics in his blood. Jimi Hendrix, the greatest guitarist in the history of rock, asphyxiated on his own vomit after an overdose of sleeping pills. The Grateful Dead's Pigpen McKernan died of massive internal bleeding, his liver ruined by alcohol. Rolling Stones founder Brian Jones was found at the bottom of his swimming pool, his liver and heart grossly enlarged by drugs.

All of them were 27 years old when they died.

Two days after Brian Jones's death, The Rolling Stones performed at a previously scheduled concert in London. Mick Jagger dedicated their performance to their former bandmate, with whom they had split due to his erratic behaviors. After the last song, as a gesture of peace and good will in Brian's memory, The Stones released thousands of white butterflies into the air above the stage.

The only problem was that it was unusually hot that evening. Many of the moths had already suffocated in their little boxes, waiting to be freed. The surviving ones barely made it up into the air before dying and falling like dusty ash on the heads of the concert goers.

It was a fitting image—not just of the flamboyant rock 'n' roll celebrities who didn't make it, but of the thousands of young people who followed their '60s dreams to an unforeseen conclusion, fluttering and falling to a burned-out end.

Oddly enough, many of the rebels who *did* survive the 1960s are conventional Baby Boomers today. Many became part of the very Establishment lifestyle they once disdained, and now live in handsome homes on the golf course, wondering why the kids don't call.

Sixties icons who are still around are now *in* their sixties. Mick Jagger is a grandfather. Bob Dylan could join AARP if he wasn't such a rebel.

For my part, I loved the fresh air, the free inventiveness of California in the Summer of Love. I loved the colors, the new horizons, the art and the incredible, unprecedented creativity in music. But as a teenager checking out the waves and the girls on Newport Beach in 1967, I wasn't an idealist. I wasn't particularly driven by the 1960s grand philosophies or countercultural dreams. I wasn't envisioning world peace or nuclear disarmament.

I wasn't thinking I was stardust, or golden, or that I had to get myself back to the garden, as Joni Mitchell's song put it. No, the '60s slogan that made the most sense to me was "Never trust anyone over 30." My experience of my mom's lifestyle and the behavior of most of her former husbands had shown me the sense of that. After all, I had rebel DNA, so the tone of the times appealed to me.

Notes

1. "The Hippies," *Time*, July 7, 1967. http://www.time.com/time/magazine/article/0,9171,899555,00. html (accessed January 2008).
2. John Lennon, quoted in Maureen Cleave, "How Does a Beatle Live? John Lennon Lives Like This," *London Evening Standard*, March 4, 1966. http://www.geocities.com/ nastymcquickly/ articles/standard.html (accessed January 2008).
3. George Harrison, quoted in Barry Miles, *Hippie* (London: Cassell Illustrated, 2004), p. 206.
4. Charles Manson, quoted in Martin Torgoff, *Can't Find My Way Home: America in the Great Stoned Age, 1945-2000* (New York: Simon & Schuster, 2004), p. 241.

MAYHEM AT THE LOVE-IN

I was 15 during the Summer of Love, living in Newport Beach, and one night Jefferson Airplane came to town. I wore my Nehru shirt, a few strands of beads and my favorite jeans.

I made my way into the packed concert at the Orange County fairgrounds. We had heard about big concerts in San Francisco and other places, and now it was our turn. I couldn't believe it: I was only about 15 feet away from Grace Slick. A former model, she had great stage presence and a compelling voice. Transfixed, I watched as the band sang their signature song of the summer, "White Rabbit": "One pill makes you larger, and one pill makes you small . . ."[1]

Later I discovered that the song was written as a challenge toward parents who had read their little children bedtime stories such as *Alice in Wonderland*—with its mushroom-eating scenes—and then wondered why their kids grew up to do drugs.

My mom hadn't read me *Alice in Wonderland*—or any other bedtime stories, for that matter. Yet the song sounded mystical, provocative and powerful all at once. All around me, the band and the crowd were in a connected, communal trance. I wasn't part of it, but I could see it.

I was an observer, the kid who sat in the back of the class and watched the teacher so that I could figure out precisely what would drive him or her crazy. I was the kid who sat at the bar with the drunks, watching how they acted. I was the guy at the concert who didn't quite enter into the massive, drug-fueled communion . . . but it attracted me in a way I hadn't felt before.

The band played on. "Don't you need somebody to love?"[2] Grace sang . . . and then something agitated the happy crowd. Maybe people suddenly got worried that when the music stopped, they'd be left alone—*without* somebody to love. I don't know. But suddenly the spiritual love-in turned into chaotic claustrophobia.

People behind me started pushing and yelling. Someone ripped off the guy's love beads to my right. A girl to my left started screaming. Someone else fell down, and the crowd kept shoving, scrambling, trampling right over her.

The spell was broken.

I'm gonna die, right here at this love-in! I thought. It wasn't fair: I wasn't even a real hippie yet; I was just a young teen in a Nehru shirt, checking out the scene, trying to look cool for Grace Slick.

A full riot broke out. Hippies were running in every direction, scattering like white rabbits. Out of nowhere the police were suddenly there, too. People were yelling obscenities at the officers, who had their nightsticks out. I screamed at some random person on the stage to help me—Grace Slick was long gone, too bad about that—and two guys lifted me up by my armpits onto the platform. I ran toward the back, past all the big cases for the band's sound equipment, just wanting to put as much distance between me and those wild hippies as I could.

So much for "Somebody to Love."

Already, at 15, I was beginning to see the dark side of the hippies' happy subculture. Given my experience with drunks and liars and hypocritical people over 30, I was quick to judge the hippie movement as just another lie.

Kids all around me in my area went to head shops, smoked dope and talked about finding peace, love and joy. But many of them were really just about drugs, sex and rock 'n' roll. There wasn't much real community and love for their fellow man . . . it was more just like everything else, where all people really cared about was what they wanted, when they wanted it, looking out for No. 1.

The whole counter-culture thing seemed pretty empty. But I didn't know where else to turn.

Notes
1. Grace Slick, "White Rabbit," © 1967 RCA Victor.
2. Darby Slick, "Somebody to Love," © 1966 RCA Victor.

BLANK SLATE

When you walked into the head shops in Newport Beach, they were dark after the bright sunshine of the street outside. You waited a minute for your eyes to adjust. You smelled incense burning, maybe patchouli or some other exotic Indian scent. Jimi Hendrix was over-driving through the sound system. You went into the black-lit room, aglow with iridescent posters—feeling like you were on drugs even if you weren't. I loved looking at the intricate, hand-drawn works of art promoting shows like "Big Brother and the Holding Company," featuring Janis Joplin, done by the underground artists of the time, led by the legendary Rick Griffin.

I would stare at the posters, taking in every line, every color and every perspective. I had been a fan of Rick's art for years. His comics in *Surfer* magazine were mischievous, a little defiant, with the kind of characters who appealed to me. He became art director of the magazine at age 20, and after helping to set the tone for the California surfing culture, he moved to San Francisco just before the Summer of Love.

In fact, he got the commission to design the poster for the Human Be-In that kicked the whole thing off. Rick's signature style helped to define most people's visual images of The Grateful Dead and Jimi Hendrix albums.

I had followed Griffin's art from his early days of drawing the lovable surfer character Murphy. But just as the Beatles had gone from the innocence of *I want to hold your hand* to *I'd love to turn you on*, Griffin had evolved, too. He had started with fun, colorful surf-culture art, but by now he was into LSD-fueled visions of flying eyeballs, sculpted skulls and other dark stuff.

I had loved to draw since the time I could hold a pencil, and as my crazy growing-up years had included so much time alone, drawing was my outlet. When I sketched, I could create all kinds of cartoon people, and I could do whatever I wanted with them. I could make them look like my sixth-grade teacher. His first name was John, and I unkindly called him "Toilet Head."

For some unknown reason, Toilet Head took it from me all year long. The teacher in the room next door wasn't as longsuffering. Defending her colleague, she announced to her entire class, "I'd like to take Greg Laurie and bury him in the sand up to his neck and let ants eat him alive."

I actually liked that remark; it added to my reputation as a bad boy.

My favorite way to mock people and get under their skin was through my drawings. In cartoons, I could exaggerate my classmate's big nose or sketch in the coarse hairs I'd observed sprouting from some old person's ears. When I drew my own characters, I was in control.

I was also inspired by the bold creator of Mickey Mouse, Donald Duck and all the rest of the happy inhabitants of the Magic Kingdom just down the freeway from my home. And if Walt Disney could call his kingdom Disneyland, it's no big surprise that I called *my* artistic empire Laurie Land.

It's not so much that it was an egotistical idea—though there was some of that, of course. The land I fashioned was safe and fun. In Laurie Land, no one threw glasses, ashtrays or fried-egg sandwiches. In Laurie Land, people laughed. A lot.

I had also been a big fan of "Peanuts." I was drawn to Charlie Brown, Lucy, Linus and Snoopy. I loved their world because there were no adults. You saw their legs in some of the earlier strips, but as the characters developed, adults simply did not appear.

Now that was my kind of world!

I also loved the way Charles Schulz drew. It was spare and clever, as much about what he left out as what he put in. He knew how to capture a moment and pull humor out of misery.

When I was a kid, I sometimes wrote to Schulz. I'd ask him about how he got started in cartooning, where he got his ideas, things like that. I even sent him my drawings and asked for his feedback on them.

Apparently when Schulz was just starting out, he had a harsh rejection from a newspaper editor who had barely glanced at his strip, said "Not professional enough," and rejected it. Schulz never forgot that, and always had time for budding cartoonists who sought his help.

When I'd go to the mailbox and see an envelope from Charles Schulz addressed to "Mr. Greg Laurie, 777 Avocado Avenue, Newport Beach," my heart would jump. I still have those letters, the imprint of Schulz's manual typewriter embossed on the thin white stationery, his famous signature marking the bottom of the page.

I created my own cast of characters early on, such as Goobers and his talking dog, Herman. When I was a teenager, I actually had cartoons published in *Surfer* magazine, which in Newport Beach was a pretty big deal. I created other characters to appeal to those of us in the surf culture; they had names like Norman Noseride and Clyde Dabum. For my high school newspaper, I featured myself and a friend named Tom as the stars. (We were extremely witty, of course, when we mocked the school administration.) In Laurie Land, things were always funnier, happier and better than in real life.

After our misadventures in Hawaii, life in Newport Beach was pretty good. My mother continued her usual habits, going to parties, drinking, meeting men, marrying them, and partying with Newport's in-crowd, including the legendary John Wayne.

Then she married a man named Bill, who would be her last—and longest—marriage. By now, though, since I was older and had more autonomy, she didn't play as central a role in my experience. I could get around on my own, so I was free to hang out in places like head shops and rock concerts.

At the time, we lived at a motel called The Jamaican Inn. We had a one-bedroom suite. I slept on a foldaway cot in the front room, and my mother reigned over the bedroom with Bill. My high school, Corona del Mar, drew kids from some pretty wealthy backgrounds. Some of them drove Porsches or Mercedes to school. And here I was, sleeping in a fold-out bed in a hotel room—and not a nice one at that.

I watched how those kids dressed, acted and talked. I figured out how their culture worked, and I set about becoming part of the popular crowd, the jocks and cheerleaders. At the time the guys wore preppie, conservative khakis and Izod shirts. I got a busboy job in a restaurant at night so I could buy clothes, and I carefully pressed my two pairs of khakis and my three knit shirts, which I wore with my cream Sperry topsiders or navy Vans canvas shoes. I carefully mixed and matched my little wardrobe so that I never repeated during the week.

One time I was visiting a friend from an affluent family, and I saw he had six pairs of Vans in different colors. He also had a mom and dad who were married to each other and who kept up with all his activities.

I couldn't imagine such a life.

Because I was funny and had a sort of cynical sophistication, the in, upper-class crowd welcomed me even though I was a lowly freshman. Next thing I knew, I was drinking and smoking at parties in Palm Springs. I hated the taste of alcohol, so I drank screwdrivers for the taste of the orange juice and the effects of the vodka. It made me feel more outside myself, less an observer and more a participant, though it gave me a dizzy, sick feeling.

This phase didn't last long. When I got outside myself, I could see the whole scene: There I was at some party, trying to get the girls to laugh and the guys to think I was cool, standing under a palm tree with a drink in one hand and a cigarette in the other. I looked just like my mom.

I was on a slick road toward a future I'd already seen.

Strangely, even though I was a cynic, I was also a romantic, hoping that whatever came next would somehow be better. In some ways I was a blank slate . . . or maybe a sponge. I absorbed whatever was going on around me. Then, when I realized it wasn't worth it, I searched for something new, something that would really make sense. I just didn't know what it was.

I decided that drugs would be my means of finding it.

ALTERED STATES

All my life, I had been hyper—constantly joking, tapping my foot, drumming my fingers, full of creative energy. But this was the late '60s, and the mode was mellow. A lot of my friends in Newport Beach were laid back, and I wanted to be more relaxed, like them.

While most of the kids at Corona del Mar High School were using their country-club parents' drug of choice, alcohol, a growing number of the earnest youth at Harbor High were doing drugs. I decided to get by (and get high) with a little help from my friends there.

So I transferred to Harbor High. My mom didn't care where I went to school. She was mellow in a different way.

I didn't want to become a drug addict. I just wanted to smoke pot and ultimately try LSD. That was how I was going to become a different person—more like the Beatles, less like me.

I loved the Beatles' harmonies, clothes and hair. I was open to the Eastern mysticism thing that George Harrison was into, but it was the mind-expanding powers of hallucinogenic drugs that I really thought would change me. My consciousness would swell and lift me like a hot-air balloon, and I would gently rise and take hold of the great starry secrets of life, love and the universe.

Like wow, man.

I grew my hair long and got rid of my topsiders and collared shirts. I was dismayed to discover that hippie clothes were even more expensive than preppie attire, but I managed to get the ruffled, blousy "poet shirts" that were big then, with jeans and beads. Like most people I knew, I had a vest with a few carefully chosen buttons: peace symbols, "Make Love, Not War," and other deeply philosophical, psychedelic slogans.

My once-clever world of Laurie Land was supplanted by drawings of magic mushrooms and marijuana plants. There were no more funny characters with punch lines, just little dull images drawn all over the page. During lunch period at school, my friend Jim and I would sneak off campus to his house, smoke some weed and come back. It seemed like everyone I knew was smoking grass, but only a few had experimented with LSD. I decided it was time for me to go to that next level of consciousness, so to speak.

LSD is made from the lysergic acid that comes from ergot, a grain fungus that grows on rye. It was first synthesized by a Swiss chemist named Albert Hofmann in 1938. When he tested it on himself, Dr. Hofmann spent several hours convinced that his next-door neighbor was a witch, that he was possessed by a demon, that his furniture was threatening him, and that Albert Einstein was chasing him with a kitchen knife. Later he saw kaleidoscopic images that exploded into colored fountains. He could see sounds and hear colors mushrooming through the sky. LSD is wacky brain fungus.

After Dr. Hoffman recovered from his trip, scientists began to explore the drug as a possible treatment for schizophrenic patients (but only those who were not already afraid of furniture or Albert Einstein). The CIA and British intelligence service hoped LSD would be helpful for interrogation of Cold War enemy agents.

But LSD took off on American college campuses, aided by champions like Dr. Timothy Leary and Dr. Richard Alpert. Leary and Alpert veered away from academia (Leary was helped along by being dismissed from Harvard) and became countercultural gurus, appearing at love-ins, be-ins and all kinds of other ins, proclaiming the glories of hallucinogenics as the path to spiritual enlightenment.

LSD was banned in the U.S. in October 1966.

But it was still available. Underground chemists produced it in crystalline form, then mixed the crystals with solutions and soaked perforated blotter paper in the liquid. A typical page had 900 one-quarter-inch squares on it, each tab sufficient for about an eight-hour magical mystery trip. When you licked the tab (or ate it), the lysergic acid diethylamide bound to the serotonin receptors in your brain, exciting layers IV and V of your cerebral cortex.

In my case, the agitation of layers IV and V of my cerebral cortex did not lead to spiritual enlightenment.

I decided to take my first hit of acid at a carnival, of all places. At first, things just seemed out of focus. Then it was like still drawings were coming to life. The sounds of the merry-go-round seemed fast, then slow. The Ferris wheel was turning and beating like a heart, expanding, contracting, then swirling and pulsing.

I was on the edge of panic, but still sane enough to hear that the carnival workers needed help tearing down the equipment that night. Always in need of extra money—to pay for hippie shirts and my new interest in drugs—I volunteered to help. I narrowly escaped being killed when a heavy crane swung down and almost hit my head. I had been oblivious, assuming it would just go right through my head with no damage to my dancing brain.

Still, I survived the night, and now I had bragging rights. I could tell my friends that I had gone on to the "next level."

The problem with LSD, in simple terms, is that it is a stupid drug. It takes its takers, making them *believe* that they are arriving at great insights. But when you come down from your trip, you realize your great insights were inane, as useful as love beads to a starving man.

My LSD experimentation was pretty brief. I soon had the quintessential "bad trip." I hallucinated that my face started melting, my bones bending. I heard a menacing voice telling me I was going to die. I could see my skull. My friends had to restrain me. They called a seasoned LSD user who came and talked me down as the effects of the drug slowly wore off.

I decided my days of tripping were over. I stuck with pot. I'd come home late at night stoned, and my mother would be loaded. We made a great pair.

Sometimes at night, I went down to the Fun Zone by the pier in Newport Beach. It was the ultimate teenager hangout, with rides, junk food and lots of kids coming and going. Often I saw earnest Christian teenagers trying to engage people in conversation.

I'd heard them call it "street witnessing."

We called them Jesus freaks.

In my mind, I associated them with my grandparents' beliefs, so I vaguely knew they were religious and had lots of rules they wanted to share with others.

There were plenty of other spiritual types out there as well, such as Jehovah's Witnesses and Hari Krishnas. The Hari Krishnas would sometimes share their food with nonbelievers like me, which was great—but I still thought they were a few clowns short of a circus.

I would lean up against the wall of a faded yellow building, stoned, a cigarette hanging out of my mouth and my long hair in my eyes. I'd see the Jesus freaks coming, talking to kids and handing out their little religious pamphlets about how to be saved. I secretly wanted them to come and talk to me . . . I was curious about what they'd say. But they never did. They'd just dart up to me like I was a dangerous dog chained to my wall, stuff a tract into my hand and run away.

I'd shove it in my coat pocket.

We were living in an upscale trailer home by the water at the time, and my mom was usually still out drinking when I got home. I'd go in my bedroom and sit on my funky bed on the floor. There were Beatles posters on the walls and a copy of the "Desiderata" poem that was so hip at the time:

Go placidly amid the noise and haste,
and remember what peace there may be in silence.
As far as possible without surrender
be on good terms with all persons.
Speak your truth quietly and clearly;
and listen to others,
even the dull and the ignorant;
they too have their story. . . .[1]

I thought it was profound, and the words were soothing, but it was impossible to live by. When I tried to go placidly amidst the noise and haste, the next thing I knew I would get angry with some guy whom I found to be dull and ignorant. I didn't care about his story.

I sometimes spread out the religious literature on my funky bed. There were little tiny Bibles with red covers. They had verses on each page.

"All have sinned and fallen short of the glory of God."

"The gift of God is eternal life through Jesus Christ."

"For God so loved the world that He gave His only begotten Son, that whosoever believeth in Him should not perish but have everlasting life."

What did it all mean?

What was sin?

What was eternal life?

What was "begotten"?

Who was Jesus Christ, really?

I didn't know the answers to those questions. The Christian stuff seemed just as unhelpful as that impenetrable poem on my wall.

Some of the tracts were little cartoon stories about people dying and going to hell. One showed a little devil laughing at a man because he hadn't heeded warnings to repent.

I usually just tossed the tracts in the trash. I hated them because the cartoons were so corny and badly drawn, and they weren't funny.

But deep down inside, I did believe there was a God.

Sometimes I would lie in bed at night and think about death. My thinking at the time was that when you were dead, you were dead. Dust. Worm food. The very thought of not existing terrified me.

I'd look at the Beatles' poster on my wall and I'd hear music in my head. *Let it be*, I'd think. But when I tried to reflect further about the Beatles' words of wisdom, if I was honest with myself and I wasn't on drugs, I had to admit they made no sense. Let *what* be? What did it mean?

There was another song on that Beatles album that hit close to home, though. Something about a long and winding road . . . and its bittersweet chords sounded like the story of my life. I felt as though I had already lived multiple lifetimes, with parts of my childhood in New Jersey, Hawaii and places all over Southern California. Military school. Different homes, schools, apartments, hotels, trailers.

I'd gone down a long and winding road, full of tears that no one had seen.

Was it leading me to someone's door?

When I'd look at the bad tracts or listen to the Beatles and think about Jesus, I'd picture the great scene from *Ben Hur* when Judah ben Hur is watching the Crucifixion with his sister, who is later cured of leprosy. It moved me.

One time I'd been at the Lido Theatre in Newport Beach for a showing of old movies, and I saw *Ben Hur* for the tenth time. I came out of the theater and some Jesus people were hanging around on the street, handing out their sorry little tracts. For the first time, I made the connection: *Oh, they follow Jesus. That historical Jesus who was in the movie. A real person.*

I was really drawn to Jesus. After all, in all the movies Jesus was a brave hero who gave Himself for others.

I just didn't get His people.

Note
1. Max Ehrmann, "Desiderata," © 1927.

1 5

JESUS PEOPLE

As the hippie scene unfolded in Southern California, a new movement grew out of it. The flower power, be-in thing had started with peace and love, but some people were becoming disillusioned. Many who started on pot and LSD were graduating to mescaline and heroin. Too many of them died, desperate and alone, with dirty needles stuck in their arms. In Haight-Ashbury, the ratio of men to women was 5 to 1: Young girls who ran away from home could count on a warm reception there, but they found out that free love wasn't so free. Gentle girls still in their teens were waking up to discover they had syphilis. Things could get ugly on the street.

Meanwhile, drug guru Timothy Leary was still touring the country saying things like:

> By "turn on," I mean . . . get in touch with your cellular wisdom. Get in touch with the universe within. The only way out is in. . . . Find the wisdom within, hook it up in a new way, but above all, detach yourself.[1]

When Timothy Leary's cellular processes eventually began to betray him due to prostate cancer, he went to his death in 1996 still convinced of the truth within. In his final days, Leary made elaborate plans to turn his own death into a public event. White-haired and gaunt, he said he felt thrilled to learn he was dying, calling death "the final party"—a team sport, like living. Three weeks before he died, Leary abandoned his plans to have his body frozen in cryonic suspension, which he had considered his duty as a "futurist." Instead, seven grams of his cremated ashes were shot into outer space on a Pegasus rocket, which orbited the earth for six years until it burned up in the atmosphere.[2]

Many hippies, however, got out of Leary's orbit back in the 1960s. His message wasn't very practical, and his drug prescriptions weren't helping them find lasting peace. They started to look up and out, rather than further inward.

They already thought Jesus was cool, with His long hair and countercultural approach that had shaken up the Establishment of His day.

As the Byrds sang on the *Ballad of Easy Rider*, Jesus was just "all right."

"Spirit in the Sky" blared from radios in Mustangs and from transistors on the beach: "Gotta have a friend in Jesus."

Songs like this weren't deep, but the point was that Jesus was, well . . . *all right* with hippies.

They just didn't know who He really was.

From a distance, the hippies who had become Jesus people were indistinguishable from any other hippies. Up close, you could see that their accessories had all been Jesus-ized. The buttons on their vests had happy faces: "Smile, God loves you." They wore Jesus shirts and their VW buses wore "One Way" and "Honk if you love Jesus!" and "If you feel far from God, guess who moved?" bumper stickers. Some of them did Jesus cheers: "Give me a J, give me an E . . ." There were Jesus posters. Jesus people played Jesus songs on their funky guitars.

Most adults from conservative churches looked on with a fair amount of suspicion, thinking it was a sham or a passing trend. For his part, Billy Graham thought that "the Jesus Movement" would become the greatest religious revival ever in the United States' history.[3]

A conservative, balding pastor in Costa Mesa, right near my home, also welcomed this strange movement. His name was Chuck Smith, and like Billy Graham, he would eventually play an enormous role in my life.

But of course, I didn't know that back then.

Notes

1. Timothy Leary, *Turn On, Tune In, Drop Out* (Berkeley, CA: Ronin Publishing, 1999), pp. 133-134.
2. "Timothy Leary" at Wikipedia.org. http://en.wikipedia.org/wiki/Timothy_leary (accessed January 2008).
3. Billy Graham, "The Marks of the Jesus Movement," *Christianity Today*, November 5, 1971, pp. 4-5.

AN UNLIKELY DUO

Chuck Smith was 40 years old during the Summer of Love. He wore Hawaiian shirts, comfortable white pants, practical walking shoes and a perpetual smile. His hair was longish, curling up over the collar of his shirt. I thought he was cool. Not because he tried to be youthful or relate to his kids, but simply because he was authentic. He was down to earth, yet he talked about heaven.

I liked that.

Born in 1927, Chuck was a promising athlete and an excellent student; he was offered a full football scholarship to the Naval Academy. But he felt a calling to go to Bible college instead, and his devout mother supported his decision.

He graduated ready to change the world, yet encountered many years of slow growth—if any—in the little churches he pastored. For a dynamic super-achiever, it was hard. His denomination wanted him to be successful. Chuck wanted to be successful. But regardless of all the great sermons he preached and all the great contests and membership drives he started, his churches just did not grow the way he had hoped.

One day he was reviewing his sermon, feeling that it would be almost impossible for a nonbeliever not to respond. Then he looked out at his congregation and realized that there was not one unbelieving person there. Why weren't the people in his flock bringing their friends and neighbors to hear the gospel?

Chuck switched from preaching on random topics and started teaching through entire books of the Bible, in the great tradition of expository preachers. He started in the Gospel of John, and his congregation soon doubled in size. He had heard that preaching through the book of Romans would transform any church, so he began to preach on Romans, verse by verse . . . and the first thing he discovered was that it transformed *him.*

"I discovered grace," he said later. "I had been trying to serve God by works. I had been trying so hard to do everything right and obligate God to bless me. But of course, you can't earn blessings. Then I began to recognize the goodness and blessings of what God has already done."

God's grace changed Chuck Smith—and it changed his church. People's lives began to change, and they invited their friends to church so that they could hear about grace. Those friends got excited and invited their friends.

As Chuck's denomination took notice of his growing ministry, he was transferred to start new congregations and enliven dying ones. Eventually, he came to Costa Mesa. The church there was not part of any denomination. It was just a small group of believers who believed God had a plan for them.

They needed a pastor, and Chuck was their man.

Even as his church in Costa Mesa grew dramatically, he realized that his early years of dry ministry had been crucial. If he had had success in the beginning, he would have attributed it to his own abilities. But his years of failure, and his later discovery of the reality of God's grace, allowed him to stay centered on the fact that his ministry flourished because of God, not him.

His church in Costa Mesa was made up of nice, scrubbed ladies who wore dresses, conservative men who wore suits, and small clean children in their Sunday best. Many of these people had never had contact with the flower children who were flooding Southern California. And for his part, Chuck was starting to realize he had a natural bias against these kids. When he saw dirty, barefoot hippies on the streets, he wondered, *Why don't you just take a bath?*

But the fact that Chuck knew it was *God's* church, not his, caused him to overcome his natural reluctance. He led his congregation to go out of their way to welcome in the very people with whom they felt no innate connection . . . the hippies.

Chuck and Kay Smith's daughter, Jan, was dating a guy in college who had been in the drug scene and was now a Christian. Since it was Chuck's job to entertain his daughter's dates while she got ready to go out (and since it took her a while to get ready), Chuck got to know John pretty well. John was the first long-haired, hippie-looking guy that Chuck had met. Fascinated, he studied John like an alien life form.

John told Chuck stories that sounded like they were right out of the book of Acts. One night John was at Huntington Beach and started talking with several guys who were high on acid. They began to weep when he told them about Jesus Christ. They knelt in the street and prayed to receive Him. By the time John left them, they were sober, in their right minds, and saying they would forsake drugs and follow Jesus.

Another night John reported he'd been in Laguna Beach, and something similar had happened, but with a group of 10 flower children.

Clearly God was stirring His Spirit among the hippies, of all people. Chuck and his wife, Kay, wanted to be part of it. They wanted these new Christians to be welcome and comfortable in churches where they could be taught in the Word and grow strong in their faith.

Chuck and Kay asked John to bring them a random hippie who had come to know Jesus so that they could meet more members of this strange new breed. The next day, there was a knock at his door, and Chuck opened it to find a young man standing with John. John had been picking up hitchhikers so that he could talk to them about Jesus, and this hippie was already a Christian. In fact, he'd been hitchhiking so that he could tell whoever picked him up about Christ.

The guy's name was Lonnie Frisbee.

God could not have invented a stranger duo than Chuck Smith and Lonnie Frisbee.

Chuck was big and strong, with vibrant dark eyes and John Wayne-like elocution. Lonnie was small and fragile looking. His flowing shirts, long brown hair parted in the middle, and soft brown eyes made him look like most people's mental picture of Jesus.

Chuck had come from a godly, secure family. Lonnie had been exposed to sketchy, dangerous characters as a child and had gotten into the drug culture in his teens.

Chuck had received Christ at his mother's knee. Lonnie had come to faith in Jesus on the street after coming off an LSD trip.

Chuck had sound theological training and years of pastoring behind him. Lonnie's spotty high school education had left him barely able to read and write.

Though they looked conservative on the outside, Chuck and Kay Smith would show themselves to be radical on the inside. They invited Lonnie to move in with them. Within a few days, he had brought some friends who had just come to faith, and the Smith house was full.

"Honey," Chuck said to Kay, "this isn't going to work. We're not ready to be a hippie pad."

But Chuck realized that many of the new hippie believers needed a safe place to live. Once they came to faith, it wasn't a good idea for them to go back to the streets or to the drug-infested communes they'd lived in before. So the Smiths' church soon rented a little house; within a week after Lonnie and some of the other leaders had moved in, 21 young men had received Christ and moved in, too. Church volunteers built bunks in the garage; one kid was even sleeping in the bathtub.

On Sunday mornings, Chuck Smith preached; on Wednesday evenings, Lonnie Frisbee drew in young people for Bible study. Church attendance at Calvary Chapel skyrocketed . . . and it looked like no congregation anyone had ever seen before. Barefoot hippies sat on the floor, praising the Lord, while old ladies in hats smiled, shrugged, and sang their hymns.

Lovesong, a Christian musical group that grew out of the church, captured the feeling of the time in their song "Little Country Church":

People comin' everyday from miles around
For meetin's and for Sunday school
And it's very plain to see
It's not the way it used to be
Preacher isn't talkin' 'bout religion no more
He just wants to praise the Lord
People aren't as stuffy as they were before
They just want to praise the Lord
Long hair, short hair, some coats and ties
People finally comin' around
Lookin' past the hair and straight into the eyes
People finally comin' around[1]

At the time, I didn't know about any of this. I also didn't know that Chuck and Kay Smith were praying for the lost kids they saw at the beaches, milling around on the streets. My little gang of friends hung out a block away from the Smiths' home. When Kay saw us slouching past their house, stoned, she prayed that God would touch us.

I didn't know that God was already at work in me. He was also protecting me, both when I had no idea I needed protection, and other times when I was scared to death and calling—briefly—out to Him.

One rainy night, I was with three friends, careening along Pacific Coast Highway. My buddy Jim was driving his mom's green 1964 Volvo sedan. She was either incredibly naïve and oblivious to loan it to us, or incredibly cynical. Maybe she just did not care that we were packing a bunch of marijuana in her trunk. We were all stoned, particularly Jim, who was (unfortunately) driving.

I felt guilty about the big wad of weed, but I justified it because we weren't going to sell it. After all, we weren't drug dealers. (I had heard early on that you could get a lot of money if you hooked up with local Mafia characters and sold pot for them. It may have just been a rumor, but it frightened me. We weren't underworld types. We weren't into drugs for profit. No, we were on a path to *self-discovery*, of course. We were not going to sell that load of weed. We were going to smoke it. All of it. Ourselves.)

We were flying along just fine, on a narrow part of the highway with steep cliffs on one side and the ocean hundreds of yards below on the other.

Suddenly the car hit a slick section of wet pavement. It fishtailed, then spun. My head whirled; we were out of control, with lights flying by and the screech of tires. All I could think was, *This is it. This is how it ends for me.*

With my cartoonist's mind, I could see the headline in the newspaper the next morning: DRUG DEALERS KILLED IN SOLO SPINOUT ON PACIFIC COAST HIGHWAY. I could see upstanding citizens like Ward and June Cleaver reading their morning paper over crisp toast and hot coffee, shaking their heads and saying, "You know, dear, it serves those deviants right." Then they'd just shrug and turn to the next page.

But I was not a drug dealer. I didn't even consider myself a drug user. I was just on a journey, and pot was helping me along the way . . . that's how I justified it, at least.

All this happened in a second. But my headline fear revealed what I knew deep down inside: This was not the way I wanted to live, and certainly not the way I wanted to die.

I offered up a tiny, feeble prayer.

"God, please get me out of this! If You do, I will serve You, or do whatever You want. Please!"

The car suddenly corrected itself. Jim braked a little, we all laughed with relief, and then we were on our way home. I exhaled, and prayed again: "Whew, thanks, God, see You next crisis!"

I continued on my merry way. But it wasn't fun anymore. Some of my friends were trying other types of drugs now, including a more potent form of LSD called STP. It was named after the motor oil, and its effects were worse than if you just went out to your car and swallowed a quart.

It was time for a change, but I didn't know where to turn. I didn't want to go back to the preppie social life of Corona del Mar. And even though I was a long-haired liberal hippie—pro-drugs, pro-sex and pro-rock 'n' roll—I felt like I didn't really fit the drug culture either.

I could even see that my quest to become mellow had not worked. Drugs had actually sapped my creativity. My art and comics weren't as sharp; my sense of humor wasn't as quick. I was apathetic, unmotivated. If this was mellow, it wasn't good for me.

But what could I do? Where could I turn?

My mom? School? God?

I liked the idea of Jesus as a hero, but I certainly had no intention of becoming a Jesus freak. That was not even on my radar screen.

I didn't think much about the Jesus people as any big cultural movement. I saw kids around town or at my school handing out their religious tracts, and they seemed like pretty harmless fanatics. As a professional observer, I was always skeptical of anything that could pull people outside themselves. Even though I was using drugs for that precise reason, I still maintained a skeptical distance from people who completely lost control. That's one reason I didn't like alcohol: Way too many times, I'd seen it make people do things they would never do otherwise.

So when I saw Jesus freaks approaching random strangers, grinning like they were happy and they wanted other people to be happy too, I was suspicious. *It must be a sham or a scam . . . nothing good could make people so free from caring what other people thought of them. They're probably brainwashed. Poor things.*

It was wonderfully ironic that God used the very guy who became one of the media's initial focal points of the Jesus Movement—besides Jesus, I mean—and one of the most controversial figures of the day to draw me to faith.

Lonnie Frisbee.

Note
1. Chuck Girard and Fred Field, "Little County Church," © 1971 Dunamis Music, c/o EMI Music Publishing, Inc.

THE REAL THING

When I wasn't sneaking off campus to smoke pot, getting in trouble for disrupting classes or drawing subversive cartoons, I was scoping the halls at Harbor High. There was a girl who'd caught my eye. I'll call her Sandy. It wasn't that she was a beauty queen, but she had a glow that I hadn't seen in other girls. She just seemed happy; there was something magnetic about her.

My invisible chick antennae were always swiveling, checking, calibrating to see if Sandy was nearby. One day I was walking to one of my classes, and there she was. The magnetic force pulled me . . . and then I saw the big leather Bible stuck under her arm.

Oh, no! I thought. *She's one of those . . . those . . .* Jesus freaks! *That's so sad! What a waste of a perfectly cute girl!*

I immediately crossed Sandy off my list of potential girlfriends. Jesus freaks were just so weird.

But oddly enough, the magnetism was still there.

The Jesus people were gathering under a big tree by the school bell tower. About 30 kids were sitting there, cross-legged, singing folk songs about being one in the Lord (whatever that meant) while a guy played on an old beat-up guitar.

I prided myself on my album collection and knowledge of rock music. I paid attention to lyrics, melody, chord changes . . . everything. I didn't just *listen* to music; I *felt* it, down deep. Let's just say that these songs the Jesus people sang did not have a whole lot of complexity. There were about four chords. Simple lyrics, repeated again and again.

In spite of the simplicity—or maybe because of it—the songs intrigued me. The kids weren't singing for themselves; it seemed like they were singing *to* someone. That was strange.

I sat at a safe distance, far enough away so that no one could possibly think I was connected with the group. That would be social suicide. But I was close enough to eavesdrop.

Other students walked by and snickered. Even when the skeptics cussed and said some pretty loud, obnoxious things, the kids on the lawn just kept singing. They really didn't seem to care what other people thought. They didn't seem self-conscious. They seemed like they were focused on something the rest of us couldn't see. It struck me that this was what kids at hippie love-ins aspired to, but never reached. I wondered if the fact that these teenagers seemed so sincere—and so secure—was because they had somehow found the real thing.

Then one of the guys in the group stood up. He had a Bible in his hand, and shoulder-length dark hair and a beard. His brown eyes blazed.

It was Lonnie Frisbee, and he'd come to teach a Bible study to the kids at Harbor High that day.

He read a little bit from the New Testament, and then he talked about how Jesus wasn't just some far-off, far-out historical figure. How He was real. How He could be known personally.

I sat transfixed. This guy looked like a biblical character, and he related to me at that moment in my life.

Then Lonnie said something that struck my heart.

"Jesus said that 'You are either for Me, or you are against Me.' There's no middle ground with Jesus. You're either for Him or against Him . . . which side are you on?"

I'd never heard it put that way. Jesus was just all right with me, sure, and I liked His stuff about brotherly love and doing good. But I'd never thought that Jesus was actually real, relevant and right there with people, wherever they were. I'd never thought that I had to make a decision one way or the other about Him.

I looked at the Christian kids, sitting there, Bibles in their laps. They didn't care what other people thought. They'd made their choice. They were *for* Jesus. No doubt about that.

Then—for once in my life—I stopped observing others and turned my objective focus on myself. It was clear that I wasn't one of those Jesus people. Did that mean I was *against* Him?

I was still trying to absorb that disturbing new thought when Lonnie Frisbee told the group, and those standing on the fringes, that anyone who wanted to decide to be *for* Jesus should come forward and he would pray with them.

My mind kaleidoscoped through my years of lost loneliness, broken homes, the empty promises of drugs and alcohol, the tantalizing search for something that I knew was real but could never quite find. *I want to be for Jesus, not against Him,* I thought. But it was too good to be true. *What if it's not real? What if I just can't do it right? What if it works for everybody* but *me?*

But I was willing to try. My body somehow acknowledged what my spirit was feeling, and before I even knew what I was doing, I walked forward to the Jesus freak preacher and stood with a handful of other students who had also been moved by his message.

Lonnie led us in a prayer. I repeated his words, asking Jesus Christ to come into my heart and forgive me of my sins.

The prayer ended. I stood there, not really feeling anything. Other people were crying and hugging. But I felt no spiritual connection, no wave of warm emotion, no tears, no big deal. I dropped my head.

It was a Charlie Brown moment.

Good grief! I thought. *Everyone can get saved except me! I can't even commit myself to follow Jesus Christ right.*

I was convinced that God had turned me down . . . except there was one thing that I did notice. It wasn't dramatic, but it was real. I felt as though a weight had been lifted from me. It was odd, because I hadn't been conscious of burdens I was carrying around. I had felt pretty free before.

But now I realized I hadn't been free at all. I'd been schlepping along with invisible bowling balls chained to both ankles. I had been dragging guilt and fear behind me for a long time. I'd had a cold core of gray fear in me since I was a small boy, cowering in my bed and waiting for my mother to come home and the fighting to start.

I'd been dogged by guilt as well. I'd been raised without many moral guidelines, but deep down inside I knew right from wrong. All the wrong things I'd done—but more than that, the *wrongness* of my selfish heart—had accumulated into a heavy weight of guilt I'd never even known I had.

Now the fear and guilt were going . . . going . . . gone. I felt unusually light.

The school bell rang. Lunchtime was over.

The Jesus people began to disband. I saw the glowing girl, Sandy, making her way toward me.

She threw her arms around me. "Praise the Lord!"

I hugged her back. *I like Christianity!* I thought.

But a day or two after my conversion, I was wondering if I'd made a big mistake. The Christian thing was so new and different, and my whole identity was wrapped up in my old life. I decided to go off with my friends for the weekend in the woods to try to sort things out.

To help my sorting ability, I brought a big stash of pot with me. We drove up to the entrance to the forest, parked, and walked into the woods, prepared to get back to nature and become one with the universe.

Some of the other guys who had some LSD with them walked a little farther, but I stopped and climbed up on a big, smooth-topped rock.

I sat on it with my legs crossed, trying to sort out what had happened to me on my high school campus.

I got out my pot and my pipe.

But then I had an impression. It was not a voice, really, but in another way it was. The same voice I had heard at my school, calling me to faith.

It was like a quiet yet strong influence inside of me, saying, "You don't need that anymore."

I looked around. No preacher had told me to flush my drugs down the toilet; nobody had told me what I was supposed to do and not do now that I was a Christian. That sunny day in the woods it was somehow clear to me that this new venture wasn't about rules I had to follow. It was about a *relationship* with God, and now He was speaking to me.

I whispered back to Him, in my soul.

"God, if You're real, You're going to have to show Yourself to me. I want to follow You, but I don't know how."

I got off the rock, took my pipe and my pot, and threw them as far as I could, deep into the woods.

Then I turned around and went home.

The next Monday, I heard that the Jesus people were meeting for a Bible study in one of the classrooms after school. I wasn't sure what to expect, but I'd already taken the plunge, so I could certainly show up in a little meeting and see what these people did when they got together.

I edged in the doorway . . . and my worst fears came true.

A guy I didn't know came up to me, slapped me on the back and shouted, "Praise the Lord, brother!" Behind him, a bunch of other Jesus freaks were all looking at me with a strange loving look in their eyes, like I was some long-lost prodigal come home. The problem was, I didn't know what a prodigal was, and I was a little disturbed by the raw emotion of everyone's overflowing warmth.

"We love you, Brother Greg!" another guy told me, coming forward to envelop me in a big hug.

It was like I had died and gone to Mars. My own mother never told me she loved me—I had grown up without hugs, kisses, or any kind of normal affection. As far as I remember, I had never really told anyone up to that point that I loved them.

Now total strangers were affirming their love for me, and it was harder for me to process than if I'd been hated or ignored. These people were invading my personal space.

It was weird, but it was also a little bit wonderful.

The music was sort of weird and wonderful, too. We sat on the floor and sang choruses that were big on repetition, our arms around one another.

Weirdness aside, there was something very comforting about being with the Christians. Their fellowship reminded me of simpler days, back when I was living with my grandparents. I remembered looking at their painting of Jesus on the living room wall, and how I'd wondered about Him. Now I was with people who knew God . . . or were getting to know Him, anyway. I felt peaceful, fulfilled. Even though it was all completely new, it also somehow felt familiar, like I was spiritually coming home to a place I'd dreamed about but never really knew existed. I felt safe.

But back in my physical home, in the yellow trailer on the waterfront in Newport Beach, things were pretty much the same. So it was extremely strange when I went home and told my mother about my new relationship with Jesus.

CHOICES/CHANGES

I waited until my mom was sober one afternoon, and told her that I had become a Christian. She sat and listened to me, a cigarette in one hand and a drink in the other. It was the drink before the real drinking began. She was still lucid.

I told her that she was living a sinful life and that she needed to stop drinking and get right with God. I came to her in my newfound Christian love and let her have it with both barrels.

My mom was not easily intimidated, least of all by the long-haired, 17-year-old, newly minted Christian standing before her, who used to be her son.

"Don't preach to me, Greg!" was all she said, but she probably could not believe this had happened. She had gone to great lengths to escape the religion of her youth; she'd never exposed me to anything remotely spiritual. As a young boy I once asked her if she knew why people celebrated Easter. She told me she didn't know. Later, when I was a rebel with no interest in religion, just like her, I'm sure she was relieved.

The problem was, my rebellion against her lifestyle was now taking me to the biblical foundation she had thought she'd escaped. She did not care for that irony.

My new Jesus friends told me that when I needed something, I should pray about it. I needed a Bible, and since I was a blank slate about Christianity, I didn't have any preconceived notions about what God would or would not do. I didn't know that God probably had bigger and better things to do than to hunt down a Bible for me.

The other guys I now knew had Bibles with leather covers, or the new *Good News for Modern Man* paperback New Testament with its little line drawings to illustrate the passages. These Bibles didn't look like the dusty tomes I'd seen in my grandparents' church, next to the clunky hymnals. And my new friends' Bibles were all marked up, with highlighting, notes and ketchup dribbled on pages they read a lot. I wanted to get into the Bible in the same way.

So I prayed that God would get me a Bible. A really nice one. I had gone to the Christian bookstore and seen a black leather Scofield Bible with gleaming gold pages. It had commentary and all kinds of cross-references on its pages. It was a serious Bible, the kind a super-Christian would carry. I couldn't afford it, though, and I was too proud to ask my mother to buy me a Bible.

A while after that I called my grandmother. I'd been too tied up to see her much over the past few years—I'd been busy doing drugs and hanging out with my friends.

"Mama Stella," I told her, "something has happened. I've become a Christian!"

There was a pause while my grandmother no doubt checked the line to make sure it was really me calling. Then she shouted, "Praise the Lord!"

I'd never heard her so excited. "Pogo," she continued, "I want to get you something. I want to get you your own Bible, whatever kind you want!"

I was floored. My baby Bible prayer had been answered, and my usually sedate grandmother was over the moon, all at once.

My friends' reaction to my conversion was less enthusiastic. Especially after my change of heart on our little nature hike, when I realized I couldn't do drugs anymore, they were suspicious that I was going to morph into a full-fledged Jesus freak.

One day at lunchtime, I went over to my buddy Jim's house, which was right near campus. As usual, a bunch of our friends were there, stoned, listening to music and talking about nothing. As I started to go up the steps to the house, I was carrying a Bible that somebody had loaned me. (This was before I received my study Bible from Mama Stella.)

The loaner Bible was huge, with a heavy brown leather cover, and the owner had taken two Popsicle sticks and glued them on the front to make a cross. Even though I was excited about my faith, I was still an artist, and I just didn't want to tote that unsightly popsicle-stick Bible into Jim's house.

There was a planter near the front porch. I stuck the oversized Bible into it, right in between the geraniums and the vinca, which covered it nicely.

I went on in the front door. My friends were slouched on the sofas in the living room.

"Hey, Greg," everyone droned. "What's happenin'?"

"Not much," I said. "What's goin' on with you guys?"

"Nothin,'" they said. "Where you been lately? We haven't seen you."

"I haven't been anywhere," I lied, even though I knew I should tell them about my experience with Jesus.

"Some really great pot came in," one of them said. "Want some?"

"*No!*" I said decisively. I was surprised by my newfound determination. Now they knew something was up.

They were still eyeing me suspiciously when the front door popped open and Jim's mother came bustling in.

"Hi, boys!" she said. "What are you doing?"

Here they were, stoned out of their minds, and she was either totally oblivious, or she just didn't care.

"Nothin'," they said.

It was beginning to dawn on me that when they were stoned, these guys were just not very interesting.

"Hey," Jim's mom continued, "I found this in the planter out front. Where'd it come from? Whose is it?" She held up my tacky popsicle-stick loaner Bible and waved it in the air. It looked as big as a suitcase.

Jim and the other guys roused a bit, looking at me suspiciously.

"Whose is it?" Jim's mom asked again.

I eyed the enormous Bible, and the glazed eyes of my friends.

"It's, uh, mine," I quietly mumbled.

My friends put two and two together. "Oh, I get it," one of them said. "Praise the Lord, Brother Greg! Are we going to be nice little Christians now?"

My blood boiled. I'd always been the one to mock people, and now I was being mocked. This was new, and it did not feel good.

"No!" I yelled. "We're going to punch you in your nice little face right now if you don't shut up!"

Now the other friends were chiming in, like lions pulling down an antelope. "Oh, right, Laurie's a Jesus freak now!"

I'd been with some of these guys for a long time, and down deep, I really cared for them. But at the same time, this was a defining moment: I could choose to hang with them . . . or I could choose to follow the Jesus they were making fun of.

I looked around and saw my friends with new eyes. The drugs, the listless uniformity, the negative outlook . . . it all seemed so lame and boring. My new experiences with Jesus were altogether more unpredictable and strangely satisfying. I wanted to stay on the path with Him.

"Sorry, guys," I said, holding the giant Bible under my arm. "I gotta go. I'll see ya!"

Within just a few weeks of my conversion, my old friends had dropped me. I didn't miss their rebel lifestyle, but I wish they could have come with me into a new experience. They continued to drift along like fish carried by the current, their long hair swirling behind them.

Years later, I heard that one of them overdosed on drugs and died. I'm not sure what happened to the others.

19

PIRATE PREACHER

My druggie friends and I hadn't been marching to a big, bold, different drummer. We'd flattered ourselves that we were so cool, so mellow, so creative and countercultural. But in reality, we were just shuffling along, lock-step—lifeless drones who all looked the same, chained to our tiresome selves. Rather than leading us to creativity and spiritual enlightenment, drugs had just been a pass to a droning status quo.

It was in my new life among people of faith, whom I'd thought were so culturally lame and set in their ways, that I found freedom and—dare I say it?—fun. As people followed Jesus and were no longer slaves to addictions or themselves, they didn't become clones of one another. They actually became more uniquely *themselves*. I encountered people of all different ages, racial backgrounds and life experiences. In the church, I found diversity. It was a lot more interesting than the homogenized cannabis mush of my hippie days.

I knew that Christians had been around a long time—well, since the time of Jesus—but as far as I was concerned, I had discovered something that no one had ever heard of before. As a small boy I'd been to church with my grandparents, but all I could remember of those days were long, slow hymns and longer, slower sermons. I would fidget and draw cartoons and get disapproving glances from my grandmother. I'd made no connection with Jesus, except for the picture of Him on the wall at my grandparents' house.

98

So I didn't have any very positive preconceptions about Christianity, nor did I have any particularly negative feelings about it. I wasn't like kids who grow up in Sunday School and then rebel and don't want anything to do with faith, like my mother. For me, Christianity wasn't tied to any particular agenda or a certain brand of politics. I knew nothing about the Bible. I knew no preachers or missionaries. I vaguely knew that my Uncle Fred and my Aunt Willie were Christians and that they had a ministry to homeless people in Los Angeles, but like most teenagers, I'd been pretty preoccupied with myself. I hadn't focused on much beyond my little orbit.

Actually, there was one famous Christian I had heard of. His name was Billy Graham. I remembered watching his crusades on television with my grandparents when I was a little boy. Whenever my mother's family spoke of "Dr. Graham," it was with reverence. My Uncle Fred had received a telegram from Billy Graham congratulating him on the launching of his ministry back in the early 1950s, and he had framed it and put it on his wall.

Early on in my faith, someone gave me a copy of Graham's book *The Jesus Generation*. Though he said at one point that his main response to the hippie generation had been that he wanted to "shave them, cut their hair, bathe them, and then preach to them,"[1] he had become excited about the Jesus People and the spiritual revival taking place among the hippies. In solidarity, he had grown his hair longer, and I remember looking at his picture on the back of the book and thinking that Billy Graham was one pretty cool guy.

(What I didn't know then was that Billy caught a lot of heat for connecting with the Jesus People in a positive way. He received tons of negative mail; some of the letters included money to pay for a haircut, and others announced that donors would no longer fund his crusades. But, like Chuck Smith, Billy Graham overcame his biases. He opened his heart to the needy and seeking kids of the hippie generation. Some historians believe that without Billy's example, the young people who gave their lives to Christ during the Jesus Movement would never have connected into established churches—eventually with their own children—and the robust evangelical youth culture that developed in the 1970s and '80s would never have taken root.)

One Sunday I heard Chuck Smith preach from a passage in the Gospel of John. Jesus was talking with a woman who came to the town well one hot afternoon (see John 4). She had tried to fill the void in her life with sex and relationships with various men, kind of like my mom. But Jesus told her that if she drank of the water He offered, her deep spiritual thirst would be satisfied.

As Chuck described it, I felt my throat getting dry. I remembered the hopeless feeling of spiritual dehydration before I came to know Christ, and how I'd tried to quench that thirst with things like drugs, popularity and alcohol. They could not satisfy it.

"Anyone who is thirsty," Jesus said later, "may come to me! Anyone who believes in me may come and drink! . . . Rivers of living water will flow from his heart" (John 7:37-38). My mind, once dulled by drugs, was now firing on all cylinders with a new passion. I thought of icy, clean water on a hot summer afternoon, and the waterfall of God's love that I had begun to experience.

In my art class at school the next day, I was still thinking about living water. I started drawing. I had seen most of the Gospel tracts that believers were using to share their faith those days; many of them were poorly drawn and unappealing little booklets that any self-respecting teenager would just throw away. I wanted to draw a tract that people would keep.

Twenty-two panels later, I looked up. Somehow I'd designed a set of drawings that communicated Jesus' words in John 7 in a whimsical way that would appeal to my generation.

After school I made my way to Chuck Smith's house. It was pretty bold of me to assume that he would want to see my artistic response to his Sunday sermon, but there I was, ringing Pastor Chuck's doorbell. He grinned when he opened his door to me, and laughed out loud when he read through my little tract.

"Greg, this is wonderful!" he said.

"You like it?" I asked. I was a little in awe of Pastor Chuck.

"I love it!" he said. "We need to publish this! We've been looking for a tract that people will actually read, rather than throwing it away. This is it!"

To my shock, Calvary Chapel printed 10,000 copies of my "Living Water" tract. They ran out within a day or two. People began to call the church and ask for more. The Chapel printed 100,000 . . . and then more. I didn't know it then, but more than 2 million copies of that unsophisticated little tract would eventually be in circulation. God used it to draw all kinds of people to faith in Jesus.

For my part, I loved the incredible, brand-new feeling of being able to use my artistic skills for Christ. When I was young, drawing was my escape from the chaos of my home life. In school, I had used it to make fun of people or as subversive humor against the teachers to get other kids to see me as a hero. Drawing was a key part of me, but it had never had an outlet that felt meaningful. The "Living Water" experience gave me my first real taste of using my gifts to serve God—and I loved it.

Then, one ordinary evening when I least expected it, another gift came to my attention, one that I had absolutely no clue I had. It was a "preview of coming attractions" for what God would do in my life.

At the time, people were coming to faith in great numbers at Calvary Chapel, and the church was baptizing about 900 new believers every month at Pirates' Cove at Corona del Mar beach. I was on my way to one of these group baptisms but arrived late, after the event was over. There were still Jesus people hanging around, though, singing songs on the beach. Dozens of teenagers and other bystanders were hanging out on the rocks overlooking the cove, listening to the songs and watching the ocean rise and fall.

I went and sat down with the group with the guitars. Then something happened. My heart was pounding in my chest, and I almost felt like I was going to throw up. But it wasn't something I had eaten. Down deep, I realized that I was supposed to talk to the group about what I had learned from reading the Bible that morning.

At first I ignored the strange conviction, but it didn't go away.

I cleared my throat. Everyone looked up at me expectantly. "Uh," I started. "I just wanted to share something that God showed me when I was reading the Bible earlier today."

People nodded, waiting for me to go on.

I talked about Jesus. Because I hadn't known hardly anything about Him before my conversion, I loved reading about Him in the New Testament. I loved how real and radical He was. I loved that He had taken my punishment for my sins, and that I could live forever because of Him.

At the end of my little talk, I felt a flood of relief, and of joy. I hadn't been eloquent, but it had felt so surprisingly good and right to be sitting there with the Bible in my hand, telling people about Jesus. *Thank You, God!* I thought.

Then I was really surprised.

Two new kids had joined us. "Pastor, we missed the baptism earlier," one of them said. "We want to publicly show our faith in Jesus. Can you baptize us?"

Pastor?

"I'm no pastor!" I said to the teenagers, flabbergasted. I had no idea if I had any right to baptize people in Jesus' name, and I didn't know how to do it, anyway.

But the kids kept pressing me.

I told them to follow me to the area where baptisms were held. I wondered what on earth I had gotten myself into. But I also felt a strong sense of peace.

I waded into the shallow water, and the first brave kid came forward. I didn't quite get the technique, but I dunked him in the name of the Father, the Son and the Holy Spirit. He didn't drown, and neither did the second person.

Afterward, I looked up at the big, rocky outcropping overlooking the cove where about 40 people were watching the impromptu baptism. I felt the Holy Spirit tugging my heart toward theirs.

Like most people, I had an intense fear of public speaking. The last thing I wanted to do was to stand there and preach to a bunch of strangers. I remembered how years before, I had sometimes come to this same beach and stood in amazement as some man, inexplicably dressed in black, wearing long pants and sleeves, sweating buckets, stood on the wall in the blazing summer sun and preached about Jesus Christ. I watched the people laugh, or yell at him, or ignore him.

Now here I was, the guy who always thought of himself as cool. Was God really asking me to preach to people who would mock me or just walk on by?

At least I wasn't dressed in long sleeves or black. I had on my surfer shorts and a T-shirt. I was still wet from having baptized the first group.

I thought, *I've come this far today. Why not?*

"Hey," I called to the kids up on the rocks. "You might be wondering why we're down here baptizing people. The reason is, Jesus Christ, the Son of God, died on a cross and paid for our sins. He rose from the dead! And He's changed our lives!"

Then, much to my surprise, I called out, Billy Graham-style, "If any of you want to, you can accept Christ as your Savior right now! Just come on down here, and I'll pray with you."

Five or six people actually climbed down the rocks and came to the water. I talked with them to make sure that they had understood the gospel, and then prayed with them. To my shock, three decided they wanted to be baptized as well . . . and I didn't drown any of them, either.

It was a strange and powerful evening. By the time I was driving home, laughing and praising God for what had happened on that little beach, all I knew was that I didn't want to be a cartoonist anymore. I wanted to be an evangelist.

Note
1. Chris Armstrong, "Christian History Corner: 'Tell Billy Graham the Jesus People Love Him'," *Christianity Today*, December 2002. http://www.christianitytoday.com/ct/2002/december web-only/12-9-52.0.html (accessed January 2008).

STARVING ARTIST

I carried the Bible my grandmother had given me everywhere. I read it constantly, marking passages in bright colors and writing tiny notes with my artist's radiograph pen in the margins. I had been thirsty for so long for something that was real and true, and this was it. Though I'd never been much of a reader—and certainly not much of a student—I took notes on Chuck Smith's sermons like there would be the ultimate test the next day.

No more daydreaming in class. This was real life.

Chuck was like everyone's favorite uncle, the one who hangs out with the kids while the adults are in the other room, having boring conversations. He was old enough to be my father, but he was one of us. He'd sit on a stool, open the Bible, and tell us truths that were thousands of years old, but they weren't faded and dull. They were clear and sharp, and they cut through the clutter in my soul.

As I listened to Chuck teach every chance I could, I was building a systematic understanding of Scripture from Genesis to Revelation. As I heard the Old Testament stories of the great characters of the Bible, from Moses to Elijah, to the Gospels that describe the life and teaching of Jesus, my outlook on everything was changing. The stories were vivid and powerful, and I could see them play out in my mind's eye. As I studied the letters of Paul and the other apostles, I saw the great logic and clarity of biblical beliefs. I didn't have to check my brains at the door.

As I was getting to know Pastor Chuck and his wife, Kay, I was also spending more time with Lonnie Frisbee.

Lonnie was one of those characters in life whose whole was more than the sum of his parts. From far away he looked like a small, mild-mannered hippie. But up close, he had a powerful charisma of personality that was much bigger than his physical presence.

People from all over the area were coming to know Jesus because of Lonnie's ministry, just as I had. We followed him right into Calvary Chapel, and that's where we were grounded in our new faith. We came for Lonnie; we stayed for Chuck.

Because Lonnie was the resident celebrity, I was thrilled when he invited me over to his house one day to visit with him and his wife, Connie. It was like getting a backstage pass for a rock concert. I came into their funky little house, checking out all the usual hippie fixtures: macramé plant holders with philodendron vines trailing everywhere, stained-glass panes hanging in front of the windows, and Lonnie's detailed oil paintings of missions, such as San Juan Capistrano.

That day, Lonnie was preparing for his Wednesday night Bible study at Calvary Chapel, a weekly happening that drew hundreds of young people from all over the area. He told me he was thinking about preaching on Jonah that night. While he got ready to go, he asked me to read the Bible story to him.

I read from my Bible, nervous that I might mispronounce some of the words. Lonnie listened casually as he brushed his long hair in front of a mirror. Every once in a while he asked me to reread a passage. I couldn't believe that I was on the inside track as he prepared for his message; I'd seen how powerful Lonnie's preaching could be.

At the same time, though, I was a little surprised that this seemed to be all the preparation he was doing.

I shoved that thought back. We went off to the church, which was packed. I felt proud to walk in with Lonnie himself. He went to the front, and after the worship music ended, he gave his message on Jonah.

I listened, thrilled. But then I realized that some of his facts weren't quite right. Parts of the story weren't exactly like it was in the Bible. They were just little differences . . . but they made me wonder.

Still, though, when Lonnie finished his message and gave an invitation for people to receive Christ, dozens of kids came forward. Fresh from my experience on the beach, where I'd "preached" my little talk and people had actually received Christ, I knew that Lonnie Frisbee might be the human instrument, but it was *God* who was at work here. I had a strange stirring within me that maybe He had gifted me—of all people—to be an evangelist and a pastor. I couldn't imagine that I could follow in the footsteps of people I admired as much as Chuck Smith and Lonnie Frisbee. But, as I knew from my studies in the Bible, stranger things had happened.

As far as my mother was concerned, I was already strange enough. She probably kept waiting for my Christianity phase to fade away and for me to do something more reasonable, like join the circus.

I tried to respect her; I was learning that the Bible told me to honor my mother, and I wanted to do it—though I was not quite sure what that meant. I also hoped she would see that my new lifestyle wasn't just a fad, but a real change that was working in me from the inside out.

The problem was, we really didn't see each other very much. While I was at school, she was just waking up; by the time I got home in the afternoon, she was on her first drink and getting ready to go to work at the restaurant where she was a hostess. I was at Bible studies at church just about every night of the week. She was at her restaurant, and after she got off, she was sitting at the bar.

We were both pursuing what we were interested in, and our paths did not converge.

As my senior year progressed, I went with some of my Christian friends on a tour of Biola University, about 20 minutes away from my home. It was wonderful . . . but still being the rebel, I broke free from our tour with the undergraduate guide, found a classroom, and sat in on some classes.

For whatever reason, I didn't feel like Biola was for me at that moment in my life. There was also the little matter of tuition. I was somewhat less than a stellar student, so schools weren't lining up to offer me scholarship money. I didn't have any savings, and my mom was in no position to help me with expenses. College just didn't seem to be an option.

My main interest at that point was in learning more and more of the Scriptures. I could think of no better place to study the Word than in the "school" where I was already enrolled, Calvary Chapel.

After I graduated from high school in 1971, I was eligible for the draft. I had friends whose older brothers had gone to Vietnam, and a few had come back in coffins. It seemed there was no end in sight for this far-away war, and young men my age were dying.

Before I became a believer I had pretty common, though superficial, views. While I wasn't a pacifist or an ideologue, people all around me were burning their draft cards and marching in protests . . . but that wasn't my style. As a 17-year-old kid, I did not understand this war or its purpose.

But after I gave my life to Christ, I talked with a pastor about the draft. Following his guidance, I believed that the Bible directed me to submit to my civil government unless it was directly opposing or suppressing the gospel. So, instead of protesting or trying to get out of the draft, I figured that if God allowed me to be called, He would use me in Vietnam.

This was a huge shift in my way of thinking. Coming out of my conflicted childhood, I had always tried to preserve and protect myself—after all, no one else was doing so. It was all about me. Now, however—though I wasn't a selfless saint quite yet—my thinking had changed. It was all about God, and even about other people. I left the whole draft situation in His hands. As it turned out, I had a very high draft number and I was not called. Soon after that, the draft ended.

Meanwhile, I knew the time had come for me to move out of my mother's house and live with people who had the same desires and commitments that I did. One evening at a group baptism at Pirates' Cove, I met a guy named Kernie Erickson. He had seen my "Living Water" tract and told me that he, too, was an artist.

But Kernie wasn't self-taught; he'd been trained at the prestigious Art Center College of Design in Pasadena where the Disney people recruited much of their talent. Kernie told me that he was living with a couple of other Christian artists in a house in Santa Ana. They began each day with prayer and Bible study, and they all encouraged each other to produce art for the glory of God.

It sounded like a dream to me.

"Hey," Kernie said, "you ought to be part of it! Do you want to move in with us?"

He didn't need to ask twice. I was already packing my mental bags . . . even though I sure didn't have much stuff to pack.

My excitement about this new adventure faded as I made my way home. My mom had been drinking, as usual, so I just told her goodnight. But the next day I told her that the time had come for me to move out.

To my surprise, tears filled her eyes. She seemed shocked. After all, she had done all the leaving up to this point. Maybe she couldn't quite believe that the one man—me—who had been with her for most of the past 18 tumultuous years was moving on.

I felt oddly grown-up as I moved into my new home. It was slightly larger than a shack, but not as sturdy. My bedroom was a converted garage. The first night when I climbed into my cot, there was an enormous potato bug between the thin sheets. I must have jumped eight feet straight up. Everyone had a good laugh at my expense.

I soon discovered that the term "starving artist" wasn't just a figure of speech. My buddies and I could barely afford groceries. We lived on "bachelor goulash," a mixture of whatever we could get our hands on. Sometimes it had ground beef in it, which was pretty high up the food chain. More often it consisted of elbow macaroni, pickles, ketchup, cockroaches, prairie dogs and whatever else we could find.

I wasn't at home that often, though. I basically lived at Calvary Chapel, hanging around to do whatever odd jobs needed to be done and scoping around for food. I talked with new Christians, evangelized on the street, answered the phones, ran errands . . . and when Chuck Smith was out of the office, his assistant would actually forward some of his calls to me. I'd talk with people who had spiritual questions, or who were going through difficult times, or who just wanted to know more about Jesus.

After his appointments, Chuck would come bustling back into the office, shaking his head and grinning, wondering aloud what the callers would think if they knew that the person counseling them on the phone was an 18-year-old hippie who had only recently come to Christ.

During this time, I started teaching a Bible study in Long Beach, the same city I was born in. Now here I was, born again, sitting on a stool with a music stand in front of me that held my big Bible and my notes. Teenagers came from all over the area for the meetings, and I was overflowing with youthful energy and passion for the Lord.

The first evening as I spoke, my foot shook up and down, a reservoir for the nervous energy inside of me. Then, halfway through the service, I saw a beautiful girl looking up at me. She had dark blonde hair, parted in the middle, flowing past her shoulders. Her eyes were brown, and she had a big smile. She was sitting with two other cute girls who I assumed were friends or sisters . . . but in my eyes, she was the one who stood out.

After the service ended, I headed toward her.

I introduced myself, and found out that her name was Cathe; her two sisters were Mary and Dodie. I was sure she would be impressed . . . after all, I was the up-front guy, and I'd just given what I thought was a pretty decent Bible message. I asked if they planned to start attending my Bible study every week.

"Maybe," Cathe said sincerely, "but there's another Bible group that meets near here on Thursday nights, so I may just go to that one instead."

I was crushed. Evidently my wonderful teaching and leadership skills had just not made a big impression.

But Cathe's casual lack of enthusiasm was like waving a red flag in front of a bull. Snorting slightly and pawing my hooves, I asked if she wanted to go out for coffee and dessert.

"Okay," she said.

I had just purchased an early '60s Corvair in a faded champagne color. (This was before Ralph Nader led a crusade to get all Corvairs off the roads of America because they were improperly designed and hazardous for their occupants and anyone nearby.) I had bought the car for $225. That was about $225 too much, but I was proud of my zippy little Corvair. The only problem was that it had a manual transmission, and I was still learning to drive a stick shift. Let's just say that I screeched and rolled and ground a lot when I was working the clutch, brake and gears.

For some reason that is unknown to me now, I thought driving that car with the stick shift would dazzle Cathe and her two noncommittal sisters.

They piled in, and we made our way into a large intersection. Just in front of me, a huge tractor-trailer slowed as it prepared to turn . . . and suddenly, my body could not remember how to work the clutch, gear shift and brake at the same time. The Corvair stalled out, right there in traffic.

Caught up in the moment, I did what any manly man would have done. I let go of the steering wheel, pressed in the clutch and honked the horn, screaming the entire time.

I really knew how to impress a girl.

Much later, I discovered that my transparency actually did make an impression on Cathe. She had grown up with a father who was very reserved and dignified, and did not often express his emotions. (At least, he did not let go of the steering wheel and scream.) She actually liked being with someone who let others know how he was feeling. So God used my screaming for good, I suppose.

As time went on, I discovered that Cathe Martin had never had a boyfriend for longer than a few weeks. She had found early on that she could manipulate guys pretty easily, and as she did so she lost respect for them. She was on an unconscious search for someone who was comfortable in his skin and sure of his convictions. She wanted someone who could stand up to her, rather than a chameleon who would be whatever he thought she wanted him to be.

She says today that in contrast to her very reserved and proper father, she was looking for someone who was unconventional, who colored outside the lines.

Enter the pirate preacher.

As we spent more time together, Cathe discovered that she liked how I could make anything into a source of entertainment. I would turn up the classical music station and sing in a fake opera voice, or make up silly stories from my warped imagination. I'd always had fun popping in and out of my little alternate universe.

The very qualities Cathe enjoyed were the ones I had developed as survival skills as a boy. Back then I had to mentally escape the chaos of my mother's world, because I could not escape it physically. So I'd break out to my own world, making up creative stories, characters, music and art.

Now, because of Jesus, I was free . . . but that coping skill was still there, and it was one of the very things that drew my future wife to me. Eventually, she wanted to become a permanent part of Laurie Land.

NEW TERRITORY

Hanging out at Calvary Chapel, I often took jobs no one else wanted to do. One of those jobs turned out to be the beginnings of the church I still pastor today.

Back in 1972, the opportunity didn't look like much. But, then again, I didn't look like much either.

As the pastor-to-be, I was 19 years old with long blond hair, a reddish beard, a few sets of clothes and a Corvair that was trying to kill me.

The church-to-be was a dwindling Bible study of young people meeting in Riverside, California.

Back then, I knew Riverside as the town I had driven through on my way to someplace else, like Palm Springs or the mountains. It was hot; no beach breezes, no Coppertone in the air.

But of course that hadn't stopped Lonnie Frisbee. He'd started a Sunday Bible study that had mushroomed to 300 kids, and teenagers all over Riverside were coming to faith in Jesus. After Lonnie abruptly left Calvary Chapel to go to a fellowship in Florida, various associate pastors from Calvary Chapel Costa Mesa had taken turns teaching the study. But it was a long way to drive, and so they'd passed it to others. Because of these transitions in leadership, the attendance had declined to about 80 people.

One day a group of the young associate pastors at Calvary Chapel were discussing who would lead the study in Riverside that week. I was hanging around at the church, my drafting board set up in the corner so that I could do freelance graphics. I was also ready to do whatever no one else wanted.

Someone in the meeting thought of me. "Why don't we let Greg do it? He's available!"

Of course. I was *always* available. I jumped at the chance.

I wasn't sure if the infamous Corvair could make the trek to Riverside and back each week, but I was thrilled. I loved teaching the Bible; it was changing my life, and I wanted to connect other people with its power. So I careened right over to Riverside the following Sunday.

I walked into the little Episcopal church where the group was meeting. It was dark and ornate. About 80 kids were there; an older man who seemed to be in charge met me at the door. I'll call him George. I told him that I was scheduled to speak that evening, expecting him to shake my hand and welcome me in.

"I don't know anything about that," he said, frowning. "You can't speak here tonight!"

I felt like he was implying I was lying. It was as if I was back in school, and he was a teacher trying to bring me under control. My old teenage rebellion started to rear its ugly head.

But then a miracle occurred. *No*, I thought, *I will not storm out. I will not be sarcastic with this man. I will be respectful and humble, because this isn't about me. It's about God.*

"Well, sir," I said, trying to swallow my pride. "I'm scheduled to speak here, so you just let me know what you'd like me to do!"

I waited. He waited. The kids were waiting, restless and bored, and no one else was showing up to lead them.

"All right!" he said angrily. "You can speak tonight . . . but just this one time!"

It was not a huge vote of confidence.

I made my way to the pulpit, looked out at the once-thriving group that had dwindled, and prayed for God's help.

All I can say is that as I began to speak, we could sense the blessing of God. The kids began to sit up, listen and get into the lesson. At the end I asked if any of them might want to receive Christ, and about six came forward. They were smiling and full of tears.

Afterward they asked if I'd be back the following Sunday. I told them I was not sure. Old George came up and told me I could return next Sunday, but it would be a week-to-week thing.

So I returned to Riverside, one week at a time, over the next few months. The group grew and grew. I met the church rector, whom I'll call Father Jones. He was a nice but, to my way of thinking, rather formal and remote man, and we didn't have much of a connection. In the beginning, he hadn't paid much attention to the "church within his church" that was happening on Sunday evenings.

But then a local newspaper ran a feature story on our meeting. The journalist described it as a "happening," with every pew filled with eager young people. Because the kids were so hungry for God's Word, I had also started a Wednesday night service. I'd done some graphics and we printed up a little bulletin for our fledgling flock. In small print at the top of the left page, it said, "Minister: Greg Laurie."

Father Jones was not pleased. We had some discussions about what was going on with the kids in his building, but he seemed more interested in the fine print. He told me I should become an Episcopalian youth pastor.

I thought about it. At the time, the church was paying me $30 a week, most of which went to pay for gas. The idea of having my own office was exciting . . . but the thought of coming into the church's organization was less so.

Our Sunday night group had become enormous, and now Father Jones wanted to address the people. It was his church building, after all, but I was uncomfortable with what he was giving the kids. He tried to be hip and say what he thought was relevant, but I felt that he was compromising the gospel message.

I wanted to teach these kids the Bible. I already had an entrée with them. I had no need to be hip or relevant. In spite of my many weaknesses, I knew that the eternal truth of God's Word was the only thing that could satisfy people's hunger, whether they were young or old.

One day Father Jones, old George and several elders from the church walked into the office at Calvary Chapel Costa Mesa. I was happy to see them.

"Hi, what are you guys doing here?" I asked.

"Oh," they said. "We're here for a meeting with Pastor Chuck."

"Great," I said. "Can I come?"

"No," they said. "It's a meeting about you. It's time to get rid of you."

Well, at least they didn't beat around the bush.

Throughout this time, beginning with Lonnie's sudden departure for Florida, I was discovering that being in Christian fellowship wasn't all happy swaying and singing. There were real problems and conflicts and egos that could be offended.

But still, it hurt when I heard the unambiguous plan to get rid of me.

I retreated to an empty office to pray. I asked God to show me how to act and what to do, and as I was praying, a verse kept rolling around in my head. It was from Psalm 118: "From my distress I called upon the LORD; the LORD answered me and set me *in a large place*" (v. 5, *NASB*, emphasis added). I didn't know what that might mean for the future; all I knew was that I was distressed, and the only One I could call on was God.

The meeting ended. The brothers from Riverside jumped in a car and sped away.

The buzzer on the intercom rang in the office where I was praying.

It was Chuck's assistant. "Greg, Pastor Chuck was wondering if you would come to his office."

My heart sank. This was all so reminiscent of earlier days when I was called to the principal's office.

I've done it again! I thought. *I've ticked off the older generation!* I had tried to do too much, too soon, and now I was going to get expelled . . . I mean, fired.

"Come in, Greg!" Chuck said cheerfully.

Why was he smiling?

"Greg," said Chuck Smith, "we've got to get you a new church."

I didn't know what that meant, but it sounded more promising than what I'd been imagining, which was, "Greg, we've got to send you to minister in Antarctica."

A "LARGE PLACE" STARTS SMALL

The new church that Chuck Smith had in mind was not on a far-away frozen continent. He just didn't quite know where it was, because God hadn't provided it yet.

But Chuck believed that God had called me to pastor in Riverside, and Chuck knew how to pray for God to do new things.

It wasn't long before someone told me about a deserted church building in Riverside. A Baptist church had split, and both factions had gone elsewhere. When I went to see the church, it looked like a war zone. The former members had hauled away their stuff, such as pews with nice brass nameplates that told who had donated them, and memorial hymnbooks and chandeliers. The pulpit was still there.

Could this be the "large place" I had read about in the psalms?

It was for sale, and Chuck Smith set up a meeting with the realtor, who wasn't exactly trying to hold on to the white elephant of a building. As Chuck and the realtor huddled, I walked through the bombed-out sanctuary, thinking about the warring Baptists, Father Jones and my group of new believers. In many ways I felt like an imposter. I was 20 years old. I had only been a Christian for three years. I knew God had gifted and called me to preach and teach . . . but how in the world could I be a pastor?

Chuck called my name. He and the realtor were shaking hands. Chuck pulled out his checkbook, wrote a check, handed it to the agent and grinned at me, his dark eyes dancing. "Well, Greg," he said, "you've got yourself a church."

He had made the deposit and the first payment for month number one. The rest would be up to me and my congregation of young people from the weekly Bible study. None of us had any money besides what we spent on gas and goulash.

I made an appointment with Father Jones and told him about my plans to move. God had already been building up a new church—a body of believers—and now we had a new building that we could meet in.

Father Jones looked sternly at me through his glasses. He was not happy. "You're going to fail," he said flatly. "The only reason all those kids come to the Bible study is because their parents know there are adults here to chaperone them. They won't let their kids come if you're just a big gathering of young people."

My heart sank. He was probably right.

But then I remembered that if I had listened to Father Jones's crony, old George, I never would have even led the study the first night I came to Riverside. I had to continue to believe that God was leading me, even if it all felt uncertain and intimidating. These kids needed to be taught the Bible, and they needed a chance to flourish.

I wanted to say something sharp that would cut Father Jones down to size, but that was the old Greg at work. *Try to put yourself in his shoes*, I told myself. I didn't even know what kind of shoes Father Jones had on. But God was working in me. "All right," I said slowly, breathing deep. "I respect your opinion. We'll just have to see what God does!"

Father Jones's pessimistic perspective made me all the more determined to take up this opportunity, even though I had plenty of inner doubts about my ability to do anything except make a mess of it.

The following Sunday evening, we announced to the Bible study that we were moving to our new location. Three hundred excited people were crammed into the Episcopal sanctuary, and they erupted into spontaneous applause. Afterward, many told me that they'd be at the new church the next Sunday.

It was a long week. I had mental pictures of myself preaching my first official church sermon to myself and three friends. And the three friends were tentative.

The following Sunday, more than 500 people arrived at our new little church. Father Jones was one of them. Maybe he came to watch me fail. Maybe he'd had a change of heart and came to cheer me on. I'm not sure . . . but surprisingly, by the grace of God, I had determined that I needed to forgive and respect him. I had him stand before the new congregation and thanked him for his role in our new church. (I didn't say what that role had been.) Everyone applauded.

The oldest person in our congregation was in his late 20s. As time went on, a couple brought up the need for a children's ministry. "We only have one kid!" I pointed out helpfully. And as the kid happened to be theirs, I suggested that *they* oversee the development of our Sunday School. They did.

Soon a godly, middle-aged man named Keith Ritter became part of our fellowship. I had told the teenagers and converted hippies that we wanted to have "an outreach to older people" on Sunday mornings. That meant people over the age of 30. Wearing a tie and looking the part of an "older person," Keith preached on Sunday mornings, and I did so on Sunday and Wednesday evenings.

We soon had a thousand people, then 2,000 in our evening meetings, but the Sunday morning was staying quite small. Yet I felt unqualified to undertake it. It was great to have Keith there; older people could relate to him better then me, a long-haired guy in my 20s.

Then Keith had a heart attack. Thankfully he survived, but he needed to cut back on his schedule. Though the young people in our fellowship all called me "Pastor Greg," a name I was vastly unqualified to have, at least I felt like I was in my element leading them. But now I needed to preach on Sunday mornings in front of adults my mother's age (though, rest assured, my mother never came anywhere near the place). I knew I was unworthy and unqualified to stand in the pulpit.

God was bringing me along a step at a time. Ever since my experience leading people to Christ in Pirates' Cove, I had wanted to be an evangelist. But I needed the tempering, accountability and week-in, week-out work that come with pastoring a flock of people through the ups and downs in their lives.

And I was really starting to love these people.

Within a year, we were meeting in Riverside's downtown civic center, the Municipal Auditorium. It had no air conditioning, and during the sweltering inland summers we roasted like ducks. We called it the "Riverside Municipal Microwave Oven." (This was new technology at the time.) But our flock of roast ducks kept growing, week by week. I couldn't explain it. As Warren Wiersbe has said, "If you can explain it, then God didn't do it." God did it.

Another thing I could not explain was my growing relationship with Cathe.

Because we are both strong-minded people, we'd had our disagreements. These sometimes escalated into full-blown arguments that ended with us breaking up, saying we never wanted to see each other again. We did this three times in three years; it became an annual event.

During one of these break-ups, my roommate at the time found out and asked me how I was feeling about our relationship. I told him that we had broken up, though I still pined for Cathe and hoped for reconciliation.

He then proceeded to call her up and ask her out! He had a nice car and went out wearing a crushed velvet suit to squire Cathe about for the evening.

Meanwhile, my clothes were vintage vintage, and after an unfortunate crash, my car's headlights were out of alignment. I was driving a cross-eyed Corvair. But in the end, Cathe and I knew that God had chosen us for each other, and we were ready to forsake all others . . . and their cars.

Cathe's parents were understandably concerned about my background. Mr. Martin was an executive with an oil company, and they had lived all over the world. They had had servants abroad, and Cathe had grown up quite comfortably. Knowing that my mom had been married and divorced seven times, Cathe's parents wondered how in the world I would know how to be a good husband. They didn't want their daughter drawn into a family plagued by such dysfunction.

I understood the Martins' feelings. But Cathe and I knew there was hope for our union, because we had a solid foundation, one that my mother had never relied on. Cathe captured it best when she sat down and wrote her dad a long, impassioned letter. They were living in the same house, of course, but she felt that she could communicate more clearly, and that he would pause to really consider her words, if she wrote out her thoughts.

"I love and respect you, Daddy," she wrote, "and I understand your fears for me. But Greg is not his mother. He's a different person." She went on to say how God had changed me and was continuing to do so. He was blessing our fledging church in Riverside, and soon I would even have a regular paycheck of some kind. She asked for her dad's blessing.

Cathe mailed her letter and crept around the house for a day or two.

Typically, her dad did not respond outright. But her mother came to Cathe and hugged her tight. "Honey, your dad got your letter," she said. "It was beautiful. We will give you our blessing."

So on February 2, 1974, in front of 500 friends, Cathe and I became one.

We were absolutely overwhelmed. So was Chuck Smith, who performed the ceremony. I'd never seen him flustered, but he must have been a little discombobulated, because when the grand moment came to announce our union, he cried out, with great fervor: "I now pronounce Greg and *Laurie* man and wife!"

I laughed so hard I slapped my leg and somehow got tangled up in Cathe's veil, nearly pulling it off.

Well, I did not marry myself, thankfully, and Cathe and I were off to great beginnings. We were young, full of energy and love, and thrilled about our future together. I couldn't believe all God's blessings in my life.

I was a pastor now, building up the kingdom of God.

But I was still a grown-up kid and a cartoonist at heart. So it made sense that our honeymoon started in the Magic Kingdom . . . Disneyland.

SOME ASSEMBLY REQUIRED

"Why aren't their beaks moving to the music?" Cathe asked.

We were in Disneyland's Enchanted Tiki Room, with hundreds of animatronic toucans and parrots entertaining us . . . but they were a bit worse for wear and weren't quite in sync with the Hawaiian soundtracks that had been recorded to go with them.

But we clapped and sang along with gusto. We were thrilled to be married and would have sung with animated warthogs if we'd had the chance.

It was the beginning of a whole new chapter of life, a chapter in which I could start fresh. I would put as much distance between myself and my mother's lifestyle as possible. I would strike the word "divorce" from my vocabulary.

When I was young, Disneyland represented a clean, happy world so unlike my own. It was full of fun, color and imagination. Main Street was a throwback to a simpler time, and the possibilities of Adventure Land, Fantasy Land and Tomorrow Land all teased a deep-down yearning I had for real adventure.

Now, with Cathe by my side, we roamed through Disneyland at the outset of our own married adventure together. We were young; our lives were before us.

We'd come many miles to find one another. We were both born in Long Beach, California, in the same hospital, three years apart. Then Cathe had traveled the world as her dad's work took his family to the

Philippines, Thailand and Kuala Lumpur. Meanwhile, my mom's restless search took us from California to New Jersey, then to Hawaii and back to California.

Then, in Long Beach, where Cathe and I were both born, we met. God had brought us together. And now we were committed to one another for the rest of our lives, through sickness, health, wealth, poverty and whatever He would bring.

As I write, we've been together for 34 years. Now we take our small granddaughter to the Enchanted Tiki Room. Stella is named for my grandmother; she looks a little bit like my mom. Her sturdy little pink self, with her bright blue eyes and reddish-blond hair, is a sweet package of history and the future, all together. As Cathe and I hold her on our laps, we laugh and poke each other and sing enthusiastically right along with the toucans; they bring back happy memories.

Little Stella just looks at us like we're demented . . . but one day she'll understand.

*　*　*

Cathe became pregnant about six months after we were married. We had little money and no insurance, but Cathe had worked for an obstetrician, and he offered his delivery services for free. The price was right.

Cathe and I attended natural childbirth classes together. I had been instructed that my role was to be absolutely silent for once, unless my wife wanted me to talk. I was also to feed her sour charms lollipops to suck on, and to help her with her breathing technique.

As it turned out, labor had to be induced. Cathe dilated slowly. Her water broke. She was trying to focus. Meanwhile, I was eyeing her candy.

"You going to eat this?" I asked.

"Aaaaarrrhhhhhhhhhhhhhhg!" she said.

I got the idea. *Shut up.*

Finally, Christopher David Laurie, all five pounds, nine ounces of him, came into the world.

I was 22 years old. I was awestruck.

In me, there was just a big blank where a father's model of experience and wisdom was supposed to be. Now I was to be this little boy's father for as long as I lived. All I knew was that I had experienced the pain of not having a father. I would do everything in my power not to let that happen to Christopher Laurie.

But how? I was an empty book waiting for someone to write the story of fatherhood for me. So I opened the one Book that had changed my life. I looked up every verse I could find on the subject of fathers. One passage I digested was Ephesians 6:4:

Fathers, do not provoke your children to anger by the way you treat them. Rather, bring them up with the discipline and instruction that comes from the Lord.

When I was growing up, there had been plenty of anger, but hardly any coherent discipline and instruction—unless you call getting things thrown at you instructive. I'd rarely been affirmed for anything I did or said. I remembered how angry, hurt and alone I had felt. So I decided to tell my young son how proud I was of him, how wonderful he was. This wasn't hard, for as Christopher grew older, I did feel this way.

At the same time, maybe I overcompensated now and then for the deficits I'd experienced as a child. I was constantly looking out for where Christopher was, what he was doing, how he was feeling. I carried him around on my back, drew silly cartoons to make him laugh, and read Bible stories to him before bed every night. I took him to toy stores, back when *Star Wars* was big the first time around, when Harrison Ford was young and Princess Leia had those amazing braids that wound around her ears.

Christopher hesitantly picked out a small action figure, maybe a little Han Solo. Meanwhile, I was standing there, arms crossed, eyeing the enormous display on the top shelf, the stuff that Christopher could not even see. I heard his little voice, down near the ground, as he held up a tiny toy: "Daddy, can I have this one?"

Then I swept the incredible, gigantic, high-tech Millennium Falcon model into my arms and brought it down to his eye level.

"What about *this*?" I shouted. "Surely Han Solo needs his spacecraft to fly around in!"

It looked as big as an aircraft carrier. His mouth dropped open.

As I played the role of the exuberant, lavishly loving father, I was unconsciously trying to make a better world for my little boy than the world I'd had. I wanted to shape his childhood as a father who was present and active in the life of his son.

But there was another dynamic in play here.

I realized that spiritually, *I* was like a small boy, hoping for a few crumbs off God's table, while His intentions were to bless me with lavish gifts beyond my scale of vision. Not enormous material toys, but gifts of grace, security and purpose that I never could have dreamed of. In becoming a father to Christopher, I was beginning to see that my own desires had been, in fact, too small—that God's grace was a huge ocean of adventures. His love was deeper than I could know, His plans for me far better than anything I could design for myself.

Christopher enjoyed—and I mean *enjoyed*—being an only child for 10 years. He paid me back for every mischievous moment in my own early life. He never stopped climbing, running, leaping, questioning. He was not a child who did what he was told the first time. Or the second. He did not inherit his mother's courteous nature. (I can only write these teasing things about him because of the stellar, godly man he is today, and because of the close relationship we enjoy. Also, he deserves it.)

A few years after Christopher's birth, Cathe became pregnant again. We were thrilled, but she lost that child in a miscarriage.

Then, in 1986, Jonathan Allen Laurie arrived. As he got older, it was clear that he had a gentle, thoughtful personality, unlike his brother or me. While we had thought that having our sons 10 years apart would preclude any sibling rivalry, it didn't quite work that way.

When you are 12, how do you get into an argument with a two-year-old?

Ask Christopher.

Who even cares what a two-year-old says or thinks?

Ask Christopher.

It's amazing how two boys can be so much alike and yet so different.

Christopher was always a lot more independent; now he puts that self-directed thinking to good use as an artist and designer. He and his beautiful wife, Brittany, are raising little Stella, whose bright energy reminds me of our boys when they were young.

Growing up, Jonathan was always more sensitive to direction then his older sibling. He has grown into a creative, tender-hearted young man with many friends and so many ways that he gives to others.

What a joy they are to me! As a fatherless boy, I never could have dreamed that I would get to be a father to two such incredible sons. But that's the kind of Father God is: He blesses His children in ways that are far above and beyond what we could ever deserve or hope for.

WORKING FOR THE HARVEST

After I'd been a pastor for a few years, I took a musician friend to eat the best pizza in Newport Beach. It was a hole-in-the-wall, with a jukebox and a mural of people on the beach. The only problem with the mural was that it was all out of proportion. Some of the swimmers were giants and others were tiny, and the strangeness of scale always bothered me as an artist.

So did the pizza. It was wonderful going down, but later the cheese made you feel guilty.

My buddy Erick and I took a table and waited for our pizza. I looked at the guy at the table next to us, and it was someone I knew from high school. He looked exactly the same, but different.

"Excuse me," I said. "Are you Sam?"

He looked surprised to be engaged by a hippie with shoulder-length hair and full beard.

"Yes," he said.

"Remember me, Sam?" I said enthusiastically. "I'm Greg Laurie. I sat near you in our fifth-period English class!"

The fact was, years earlier Sam had been a bit nerdy, and I used to torment him.

"Oh, yeah," he said. "I remember you, Greg. You were always getting into trouble and playing jokes on people and being sent to the principal's office!"

"Oh," I replied earnestly, "I'm not like that anymore. Sam, I'm not the same Greg Laurie you used to know. I've become a Christian . . . in fact, I'm even pastor of a church now!"

Sam was dumbfounded. "Really? That's, uh . . . hard to believe, but, Greg, that's really great!"

At this point, my friend Erick excused himself to go to the bathroom. In Erick's absence, our hot pizza arrived. I began to salivate, and ended my conversation with Sam. I waited for Erick to come back from the bathroom so we could get started . . . but then a devious thought entered my head.

There were two little bottles on the table. One had Parmesan cheese and the other hot pepper flakes.

Wouldn't it be great, I thought, *to cover Erick's side of the pizza with those hot pepper flakes?* He wouldn't notice them on top of all the gooey cheese . . . but then when he took a bite, his mouth would be on fire.

I smiled at my own amazing cleverness and began furiously shaking the pepper flakes on Erick's side of the pizza.

Suddenly I heard a voice interrupt my prank. "Haven't changed much, have you, Greg?"

It was Sam. I had completely forgotten about him.

I sputtered out an apology to him, but I knew there was not much I could say that could undo his impression of me and of God's work—or lack thereof—in my life.

When Erick came back, I turned the pizza around, and I ate the hot side. I figured that as I'd already eaten crow, I might as well also eat pizza with too much pepper. When I confessed what I'd done, Erick just laughed it off.

But Sam did not.

But in spite of my obvious shortcomings and the fact that I was still a work in progress, God continued to bless our work at the church. It began to take on some of the distinctions that still characterize it today.

This was in 1974, before the boom of casual worship, seeker-friendly churches and many of the outreach innovations that are common today. Back then, Contemporary Christian Music was in its infancy, but it's fair to say it was born during the Jesus Movement. And I had seen it explode at Calvary Chapel Costa Mesa.

Calvary Chapel broke the mold in its mid-week services by using Christian praise music that was heavy on guitars. Kids with long hair, shorts and sandals flooded the place. After the incredible praise and worship, we sat for an hour with our Bibles opened as Pastor Chuck, Kenn Gullicksen, Don McClure, Tom Stipe or one of the other pastors taught a detailed study of a section of Scripture.

On Sunday mornings, however, Calvary was still a traditional coat-and-tie environment. I respected that, but at our budding new church in Riverside, I wanted to do something different than I had seen in most of the Sunday morning services in churches of that time.

Because we were reaching out to young people in our little church, I wanted to use contemporary worship and casual dress not just on Sunday nights, but on Sunday mornings as well. But even though our *style* would be contemporary, I didn't want to make the gospel more "relevant" by adjusting its message. I'd seen some preachers do that and lose the gospel truth in the process. I would preach the Bible as the authoritative Word of God and Jesus Christ, the same yesterday, today and forever. I wasn't going to pursue trendy topics; I was going to teach, verse by verse, from entire books of the Bible. Then, when I needed to teach on specific issues, people would see them from a biblical perspective. My training was in expository preaching, and that was where I'd take my stand.

A friend from Riverside, Bob Probert, was my worship leader and associate pastor in the critical first days of our ministry. Another friend, Rick Thompson, was also involved, and later went on to form a contemporary Christian music band. The church was bursting at the seams, and we couldn't have been happier.

It's been said that the job of a preacher is to get the cookies onto the lower shelf where the children can get to them, and Bob and Rick freed me to immerse myself in the study of God's Word so that I could make the Bible accessible to the young people who were coming to our church for cookies.

Because many of the kids brought their parents with them, we had to blow out back walls to add more seats. We expanded to three over-flowing services on Sunday mornings and two on Sunday evenings. A flourishing "Through the Bible" study met on Wednesday evenings.

At this point, we really needed to finalize the little detail of a name for the church. I was talking with Chuck Smith one day, and he suggested that we call it . . . Calvary Chapel!

I was surprised that Chuck would want to franchise his church name, but I was honored. The next thing I knew, we had signs painted with our new name: "Calvary Chapel of Riverside."

The first thing I wanted to do was surround myself with people whom God was calling to minister in the same way, people who were smarter and more gifted than me. I knew that ministry is a team effort, not a one-man show, and I had seen what happened to pastors who had no accountability in their lives: They blew off-course. Because I came from a life of little structure and lots of deception, I really wanted to build a ministry with strong foundations and honest communications. I knew it wouldn't be perfect—but I was intentional about how we would design it.

There was a wild group of guys who came to faith around the same time I did, men like Mike Macintosh, Raul Ries, Don McClure, Steve Mays and Jeff Johnson. These men, along with some who would come later—like Skip Heitzig, Joe Focht, Bob Coy and Damian Kyle—were a "band of brothers" to me.

Today we have well over 30 years of history together. We knew one another when we were nobodies. Today we know we're still nobodies, in spite of how large our churches may have grown. We can still let our hair down—those who still have hair, that is—and speak to each other in blunt love, as brothers speak to brothers. That is a good thing.

Back when our church was beginning, I was a peculiar combination of the studious, disciplined pastor, and the young guy who was overflowing with exuberance. One day my exuberance expressed itself when one of our friends left his Mini Cooper in front of the church.

After he left, a few of us looked at each other, nodded, and went outside. We picked up the tiny car and carried it into the sanctuary, all the way to the front. When our friend came back, there was his Mini Cooper, sitting in front of the pulpit like it was waiting to be baptized or something.

Another day my buddy Erick, the musician—he of peppered-pizza fame—started jamming on the piano. The church was empty, and Erick was playing a heavy gospel beat. I jumped up on top of the piano and started shouting and singing like a good old-fashioned Pentecostal preacher.

"Brothers and sisters, GOD is going to move here today, but frankly, I wish more of you had come!" I roared to the empty pews as Erick pounded the ivory keys.

I was still jumping around, laughing with Erick, my back turned, when two older, conservatively dressed women slipped in the back of the sanctuary. They approached the front slowly, no doubt concerned that Erick and I had both recently escaped from a psychiatric facility.

"Excuse me!" one piped up. I nearly fell off the piano.

She continued, "We're looking for the pastor of this church. Can you tell us where he might be?"

There I was, on top of the piano, long hair hanging down, sweat on my brow. There was no way I was going to tell this nice lady that I was the senior pastor of this operation. I directed her upstairs to the offices, to another pastor who was acting far more pastoral that day.

As none of us was particularly shy, it's no surprise that we soon began to use media as another way to get the gospel message out. We launched a daily radio program, calling it *Harvest Celebration*, and recorded it in a friend's bathroom because we thought the acoustics were better there. I had a drawing board set up in my office and was still doing all kinds of graphic design to support myself (as I had no other real salary), and we put out tracts designed to tell people about Christ. Eventually we were able to get access to television programs and larger-scale public events where I preached the gospel and gave people the opportunity to publicly come forward and receive Jesus. We called these "Harvest Crusades."

We were all about spreading the seed of God's Word, watering it, and bringing people who didn't yet know Jesus into His kingdom. I liked the "Harvest" name because we wanted to be the faithful "laborers to the harvest" that Jesus talked about in the Gospels.

By this time, Calvary Chapels were popping up everywhere in Southern California, and sometimes people got mixed up about which church was which. Our fellowship in Riverside was becoming better known for our "Harvest" name because of our outreaches. So though our theology and philosophy were the same as our Calvary Chapel roots, we decided to officially become "Harvest Christian Fellowship."

One day in the mid-1980s, when we had reached around 8,000 in Sunday attendance, I received a call from a person at an organization that specialized in megachurches. I hadn't even heard the term at that point, but this man told me that Harvest Christian Fellowship, the little church that no one wanted, was now one of the largest churches in the United States.

Today we have about 15,000 members. We're still growing. We've planted other churches and have sought to influence other young people going into the ministry. One of the ways we do this is through our "Preach the Word" conference, where we gather some of the nation's finest Bible expositors to teach. God has allowed us to reach around the world with our Harvest Crusades and radio program, which is now called *A New Beginning.*

Not the sort of place you'd expect a "lost boy" to end up . . . but God is full of peculiar surprises.

COLLARS AND CALLING

Though my mom assuredly did not raise me as a Christian, she played a key role in my conversion. Because of her, I saw the world and its supposed charms. I saw secular attractions and hedonism up close. I saw what it was like to chase after your desires and gulp them down, only to find that your glass was perpetually empty, your thirst unmet.

I'd had to learn to think for myself at an early age, because my mom was often too muddled by martinis to think or act for me. What I learned was that my mother's life represented precisely what I did not want in my own.

Some kids raised in Christian homes rebel against the way they were brought up. They're attracted like moths to the flames of this world. In an oddly similar way, I rebelled against my pleasure-seeking upbringing. I yearned for something that was good, something worth pursuing, something worth living for.

My mother ran away from God to the world when she was 17. Because of her example, I ran from the world to God when I was 17.

In my early years as a believer, I couldn't quite see how my dysfunctional upbringing was part of God's plan. I just wished I'd had a family with Mom and Dad at the dinner table every night, a family where we passed each other the mashed potatoes, roast beef and apple pie, and then opened our Bibles together for family devotions.

I wished I'd had an intact family with healthy habits.

I wished I had never known the ways of the world so up close and personal.

I even wished I had a better testimony!

Here's what I mean: I was amazed and honored when I actually got to know my evangelist hero, Billy Graham. I spent time with him in his mountaintop home in North Carolina and in cities where he was preparing for a crusade, and soaked up everything I could. When I reflected on my story of faith, I thought, *Why couldn't I have been led to Christ by someone I admired as much as Billy Graham?* That would have been something I could be proud of . . . in the most humble and spiritual way, of course.

But no. I was introduced to Christ by Lonnie Frisbee, one of the most controversial and charismatic figures of his day.

Back in the 1970s, I observed that as long as Lonnie was around Chuck Smith and Chuck's systematic teaching of Scripture, he seemed to do well. But after Lonnie parted ways with Calvary Chapel, he got involved with people whose theology was skewed. It affected his thinking. When he surfaced again, it seemed as though he was trying to recapture the glory days of the early Jesus Movement. A newspaper advertisement featured a photo of him as the man who "started the Jesus Movement." That choice of words captured my concerns about Lonnie at the time. No mere man could take credit for the Jesus Movement. *Jesus* started it.

Lonnie went off track. As Chuck Smith put it later, with much love and regret, he became "spiritually sterile." Perhaps that was why he succumbed to a spiral of temptations that ultimately resulted in him contracting the AIDS virus.

My friend Mike Macintosh and I went to see Lonnie in March 1993. He was in hospice care in Newport Beach, and my heart broke to see him so emaciated and in pain. We knocked on the door and were met by his caretaker, who guided us up some stairs to a large room, where

Lonnie sat perched on a couch. Though he was a skeleton with skin, he grinned and greeted us warmly. He talked with gusto, telling us how he would be miraculously healed and would continue his preaching ministry around the world.

He was sad, though, about the course his life had taken. He told us he regretted some of the choices he'd made.

The sun set and Lonnie's caregiver lit a fire in the fireplace. Lonnie kept talking, his face lit by the warm flames. The sight took me back to camps we'd held in the mountains more than 20 years earlier. We'd build a big fire, and Lonnie would preach to all the "Jesus people" while the flames danced and the logs crackled. We were so proud and thankful that he was our preacher.

But it was different now.

The fire was so small, and Lonnie seemed smaller too, like a little boy. His life was flickering out. Mike and I hugged him, told him we loved him, and then we prayed together.

I never saw him again.

If I was writing my life story the way *I'd* want it, there would be a squeaky-clean version of my conversion. I'd be led to Christ at Billy Graham's knee. No odd puzzle pieces, no ragged edges. No controversy about Lonnie Frisbee, who 30 years later would die of AIDS.

But God used Lonnie powerfully at one time in my life; and in the end I told him so. He is part of my story. God often works through ways that surprise me, ways that I'd never choose. All I know is that He is God, and I am not.

Another part of my story that doesn't fit the picture I would have chosen is the education piece. I have only a high school diploma to my credit. This lack of credentials could be considered a real liability. After all, when I go into a doctor's office, the first thing I do is check out the diplomas on his or her wall. I want to know that my doctor has been properly trained. The same is true in churches and media ministries;

we want our pastors to have their ducks in a row and their ThDs and DMins and PhDs up on their walls. We want them to know their Greek and Hebrew, and to mind their Ps and Qs.

I was a poor student in high school. I spent more of my time entertaining my fellow students and mocking my unfortunate teachers than concentrating on the work at hand. I also spent a lot of time in the principal's office.

So when I—of all people—was converted and called by God to teach, it meant I had to learn how to study. Before that time, I never had any real incentive to gain knowledge . . . but in my new relationship with God, the Holy Spirit made me ravenous for the red meat of Scripture. I sat under Chuck Smith's teaching, absorbing not only his expository instruction about various passages but also the theological foundations on which they rested. I eagerly devoured the writings of G. Campbell Morgan, Martin Lloyd Jones, D. Griffith Thomas, H. A. Ironside, Charles Spurgeon and many others. I had never read and studied so hard in my life.

As time went by and my opportunities grew, I was able to learn in person from men I'd only read before. (Not Spurgeon—he was fairly inaccessible, being deceased.) I got to spend a lot of time with, and ask many questions of, John MacArthur, Alan Redpath, Chuck Swindoll, Warren Wiersbe, Billy Graham and, of course, Chuck Smith.

One of the strongest ways to learn is to teach. As Spurgeon said about his own preaching, "Every time I stand up to bring the Bible to people, my knees knock." It is a holy calling. So though I preach with a casual, conversational teaching style, I prepare painstakingly, studying, reviewing, praying and digesting each portion of Scripture before I presume to teach it to others.

I don't necessarily recommend my own unconventional path to preaching. I've met so many leaders who have hugely benefited from their schooling, and I'm honored to serve with them. But sadly, I've also met many with extensive theological education who are actually largely ineffective for the Kingdom, because they weren't called to a teaching ministry in the first place. I don't think any seminary can put into a person what God has left out.

When I become discouraged and wish that my educational pedigree was different, I'm cheered by the odd fact that some of the greatest preachers in history—and some of the very theologians evangelical pastors consult—did not have a formal education.

G. Campbell Morgan, whose commentaries have served generations, was chronically ill and unable to attend school. Without seminary training, he became a Congregational minister.

The brilliant preacher and writer Martin Lloyd Jones went to medical school at age 14. After completing his degree, he felt urgently called to full-time Christian ministry. He never went to seminary.

Dwight L. Moody was one of the world's most influential evangelists and the founding pastor of what became Moody Church in Chicago. He didn't attend school beyond the fifth grade. He had crude manners, terrible grammar and could not spell. He was never ordaned. I mean ordained.

One of Moody's successors, H. A. Ironside, pastored the church for 18 years. He became one of the world's best-known Bible teachers. He had only an eighth-grade education.

Charles Haddon Spurgeon was to nineteenth-century England what Moody was to the United States. Although Spurgeon never attended theological school, by the age of 21 he was called "the Prince of Preachers," the most respected speaker and writer of his day.

I'm not advocating brash manners, poor spelling or a lack of education. But the fruitful ministries of these great men show what I hope is also true in my own small case: God is not limited. He uses whomever He wills for His work, whether or not they have diplomas on their walls.

But God made sure my walls aren't bare. In 1999, I was awarded two honorary doctorates from two outstanding Christian universities,

Biola and Azusa Pacific. For me—the guy whose beginnings were marked by low grades, underachiever purple ribbons and mediocre blue stars—it is pretty unbelievable to go on those campuses and occasionally hear people call me "Dr. Laurie."

But I'm still just "Greg." And I know that God uses flawed, eccentric, failed human beings to highlight His power. That way, onlookers won't give anyone else the credit that is due to God alone. That's why He called me, of all people, to be an evangelist.

Nonbelievers have told me that when I've listed their objections to Christianity or described what they might be thinking or feeling, it was as though I was reading their minds. This is not because I am a prophet. In effect, I was reading my own mind, remembering my doubts when I first heard the gospel. I can relate with hurting people's experiences.

Growing up as a child of divorce, with the blame, guilt, confusion and hurt that entails? I experienced it . . . not once or twice, but six different times. (My mother's first divorce happened before I was born.)

Alcoholism? Alcohol devastated my youth. My mom ruined herself and most of her relationships through its use.

Drug use? I went down that stupid road. I could have been killed or could have inadvertently hurt others.

The party scene?

Looking for love in all the wrong places?

I fell into those traps as well.

So it's not hard for me to put myself in a nonbeliever's scuffed shoes. I've walked in them. I was full of skepticism and doubt; I thought I would never make it as a Christian—I did not see myself as the "religious type."

Thankfully, God doesn't look for the "religious type." He looks for the "sinner type." I qualified. And against all odds, He changed my life.

A few years ago, I was speaking at one of our Harvest Crusades in Christchurch, New Zealand. Contrary to what some believe, New

Zealand actually did exist before *The Lord of the Rings* trilogy was filmed
there. It is astonishingly beautiful . . . and, sadly, has one of the highest
suicide rates in the world. I've found that many of the unchurched people there are spiritually quite hungry.

New Zealand reporters seem to have some pretty negative notions
about religion and the clergy. They think most American preachers are
hypocritical, flashy televangelists. One reporter told me that she was
surprised I did not travel with an entourage. She was also quite curious
when she saw the song lists on my iPod. She fixated on Jimi Hendrix.

I told her that it's not like I sit around and groove to Hendrix all
day. But I do have a few of his songs, along with other old bands from
the '60s, that I listen to from time to time.

When her article came out in the newspaper, here's part of what
she said:

> The man delivering the word of God to Kiwis listens to the
> devil's music on his iPod. "Well, Jimi Hendrix is a really good
> guitar player," says Greg Laurie, music lover, sometime surfer,
> mega-church pastor and big-stadium evangelist. And it is here
> for the grace of God he goes. He dresses well, but his tanned
> face with stubble makes him look more like the guy who came
> around to fix your roof. He appears level and down to earth,
> characteristics that have seen him go from a partying teenager
> who grew up with an alcoholic mother to a man who crusades
> for the spiritual well-being of thousands of "souls."

"More like the guy who came around to fix your roof." I asked some
Kiwi friends what that phrase meant to them. It was a compliment, they
told me. The reporter was essentially saying I was an everyman. An
everyday, hardworking, blue-collar kind of guy.

God chooses whomever He pleases. Today there are lots of white-
collar preachers and evangelists, and they're great at reaching white-collar

audiences. But God appears to be using me to reach people who might not be drawn to an academic or upscale setting, people who might not have come from secure beginnings. God is using the brokenness, disadvantages and weak spots in my story to attract people who come from the same kinds of stories.

So I'm happy to be a "roofer preacher," a blue-collar evangelist in a white-collar culture. Frankly, I am more than happy to share the gospel with whoever will listen, be they white-collar, blue-collar or no-collar. For if I have learned nothing else, I have learned this simple truth: Everyone needs Jesus.

I sure did.

FROM BILLY GRAHAM
TO DISNEYLAND

In the evangelical world, an invitation to Montreat, Billy and Ruth Graham's home in the mountains of North Carolina, was like an invitation to the White House (and in some ways, even better!). During our first visit there, I was in awe as Cathe and I stood on the front porch of the Grahams' rambling cabin. The immense beams of the house had been reclaimed from nineteenth-century homes throughout the Piedmont; the setting felt comfortable, secure and established. You could see for miles in every direction. This was the Grahams' private retreat to which heads of state, film stars and leaders came from around the world.

I couldn't believe that we'd been invited for lunch with Ruth and Billy. How could my long and winding road have led to *this* door?

I looked down. I wanted to clean any dust from my shoes, which were not worthy to cross this threshold. Then I read the words on the doormat and I felt more at home: "NOT YOU AGAIN!"

The weathered door swung open and Ruth Graham drew us in, hugging us and taking our coats. We sat down at a big round table. At its center was a lazy Susan like my aunts had had when I was young. Ruth had made a savory pot roast, mashed potatoes and hot, buttery rolls.

After we ate, we helped her carry the plates to the sink. The sign over it read: "Divine service done here daily."

Ruth bubbled with joy, Scripture, wisdom and laughter. Billy looked to her more than I had realized. They were a team, two people drawn together across time to shine for God in different ways.

Because Billy was such a hero to me, I was absolutely flabbergasted the day he fixed me with his eagle gaze and said words I'd never even dreamed he'd say: "Greg, I've been thinking about you," he began.

I snapped to attention.

"I think you should leave your church and go into full-time evangelism," he continued. "I think you should do crusades with us here at BGEA."

If God had spoken to me from a cloud, I could barely have been more stunned. My life unspooled, then played in fast-forward. I saw my broken beginnings, the reverence with which "Dr. Graham" was held in my grandparents' and uncle's homes, my great admiration of Billy Graham as the champion of the scruffy Jesus People, then my increasing love and respect for him over the years as the man who shot straight with the gospel no matter where he was. I could not believe that my dysfunctional life had somehow arrived at this Hallmark moment: Billy Graham, telling me that I should come work with him?

I also could not believe my response. I had actually come to the point in my journey where I could tell the difference between God and Billy Graham.

"Billy, you know that when you tell me that, it's like Moses proclaiming God's will from on high," I began.

Billy smiled. He was humble enough to laugh at himself, and perceptive enough to know the immense weight his opinion held.

"I can't tell you how much that means to me," I continued. "But I know God's calling for me right now. It's to pastor our church *and* to do evangelism. It's not the same for everyone. But for me . . . right now . . . I need to do both for each one to be fruitful on its own."

Billy's blue eyes pierced right through me. He was satisfied with my halting answer. He nodded, smiled again, and we talked of other things.

That conversation took place many years ago, but I think of it often. God had brought me a long way.

The last time I was with Billy Graham, his son Franklin wheeled him into the dining room as our BGEA board of directors' meeting broke for lunch. Billy's eagle eyes were softer, his once-strong voice so gentle. He told us how much he missed Ruth since she'd gone on to glory. He made us laugh as he described how he'd just spent a couple hours holding the hand of another woman.

She'd been his fiancée when they were young, but she had broken up with him because she did not feel he was spiritual enough or that he would ever really amount to much! It was that very event that spurred Billy to a deeper commitment to Christ. Now, about a century later, her husband was ill, and she'd asked Billy to come and pray for him. Billy had rolled in, held her hand and prayed at the bedside of her ailing husband. After that, he'd flown to the White House. The President had met him in the driveway and, to the astonishment of his aides, pushed Billy's wheelchair around all afternoon.

Life as usual . . . for Billy Graham.

"Billy," I said to him, "that reminds me of an urban legend about you." I told him the story I'd often heard, how Billy was once picked up at the airport by a limousine. As they tooled along, Billy asked the driver if they could change places, just for a while. He'd always wanted to see what it felt like to drive a long, black limo.

The driver agreed, and they switched seats. Billy took the limo out on the open highway and gunned the motor. He was zooming along at about 85 miles per hour when a police car took notice. The officer pulled the limo over, and Billy sheepishly handed him his license.

The officer went back to his squad car and radioed headquarters. "I've, uh, pulled over a limo," he said.

"So?" barked the sergeant. "Who's in it?"

"I don't know," the officer whispered. "But it must be someone really big. All I can tell you is that *Billy Graham* is the driver!"

I told Billy, "When you were being pushed in your wheelchair at the White House, someone might have asked, 'Who is that man in the wheelchair?' to which someone else might have responded, 'I don't know, but the President of the United States is pushing him around!'"

Billy grinned. Lunch was over. I had so many things I wanted to say, and so little time. It all welled up inside, and I leaned down to say words that don't come easily, words I almost never say to anyone outside of my wife and family. I never heard them growing up. They are words I never dreamed I would one day say to my hero, the esteemed Dr. Graham.

I leaned down to look him in the eye. His silver hair shone. His eyes were clear. I felt like he had one foot in this world, the other in heaven with Jesus and Ruth.

"I love you, Billy!" I choked.

He smiled. "I love you, too, Greg."

⋆   ⋆   ⋆

If Billy Graham was my hero, there was another, far more secular icon in my life.

Walt Disney.

So it was fitting, in God's wild story of my life, that He would bring together my childhood dreams and my heavenly calling, all in one place.

Yes: an evangelistic crusade in Disneyland.

When I was a child, the Magic Kingdom lived up to its name. I went there every year for my birthday, and I remember craning my neck to look up to the lofty heights of the Matterhorn. I laughed and screamed in the darkness of the Peter Pan ride, which frightened me when I was small. I climbed to the top of the Swiss Family Robinson's tree house and looked down on the treetops of Tom Sawyer's Island. At night,

Tinker Bell flew across the dark sky, fireworks lit the pale towers of Sleeping Beauty's castle, and in the explosions of color, I dreamed that magic could be real.

Over the years, whenever I returned to Disneyland, no matter how much I'd changed, it remained the same. It was a brightly colored constant in my chaotic life.

One day after I'd been a pastor for a while, I was teaching a Bible study in Orange County. One of the participants, a guy named T.C., worked at Disneyland. He told me we should do a crusade there. *In my dreams*, I thought.

But T.C. told me that we could rent the entire park for an evening private party. That's right: All we had to do was pay the bill, and I could preach the gospel in Disneyland to my heart's content. Guests who were already in the park for the day were welcome to stay for our event, or they could, of course, leave if they preferred. This was called a "mix-in."

It was such a crazy idea that I loved it immediately. My friend Mark Ferjulian took over the planning, negotiated the contracts and booked the bands. When the day came, we had a Christian musical group in each of the park's main sections, with speakers sharing the gospel and encouraging people to come to "the main event," where I'd be speaking on Tom Sawyer's Island.

We booked Lou Gramm to sing before I spoke. Lou was lead singer of the '70s megagroup Foreigner, and he had come to know Jesus. When he took the stage, he sang his multi-platinum hit "I Wanna Know What Love Is." He was joined by a massive Harvest Choir singing the chorus, and Lou sang out with his powerful, shimmering vocals: "Now I know what love is . . . I know; He has shown me!"

As Lou's song echoed in my mind, I thought of my boyhood years searching for love and how God had changed my lonely life . . . He *had* showed me what love is. I looked at the Disney Matterhorn jutting up into the night sky and remembered the magic it had represented when

I was a boy. I looked into the crowd of 15,000 people; I couldn't believe that I had the chance to tell them about the love of God. I did, and hundreds prayed to receive Jesus that night, the kingdom of God coming down on the Magic Kingdom in a way I never could have imagined as a child.

Nor could I have imagined how God would use our more conventional outreaches over the years. I'm told that about 400,000 people have received Christ or rededicated their lives to Him in our Harvest Crusades.

Incredible.

But as our buddy Lou Gramm sang in Disneyland, that's what love is: God showing people Himself, and drawing them home. I only preach what I know to be true: just the gospel. God does the rest.

JUST THE GOSPEL

When I preach in a crusade setting—whether it's at Disneyland, Angel Stadium, Madison Square Garden or at a roofers' convention in New Zealand—or if I'm talking with someone I met at Starbucks, I don't assume that people understand biblical language.

The Old and New Testaments used to be well known, even by nonbelievers; they shaped a common understanding of life in our culture. But today, that veneer of understanding is gone. So when I talk with nonbelievers, I don't use terms like "justification," "salvation," "conversion" or "repentance" without carefully defining what I mean. I strongly believe that we've got to communicate the gospel so that it can be understood by secular-minded people. Otherwise we just end up talking to ourselves.

This does not mean that I cut out Christianity's offensive parts in an effort to be relevant. I've heard preachers who have tried so hard not to offend that they have deleted any mention of such distasteful subjects as sin and Jesus' bloody death on the cross. I'm not sure what they're preaching, but there is no Christianity without the cross. Sometimes in people's attempts to cross over, they don't bring the cross over.

Even in our most cutting-edge Harvest youth outreaches—when we've got bands that are so loud people in the next state can hear them, and attendees with so many piercings they get better reception than my TV—I don't compromise the gospel in an attempt to make it more appetizing. I talk about sin, hell and Jesus' sacrifice. Then I talk about His forgiveness, His power and how He rose from the dead and lives in heaven today. And the young people of the iGeneration don't just yawn and text their friends. They are cut to the heart. They come forward, in tears, to receive Jesus.

Last time I spoke at Angel Stadium in Anaheim, California, 102,000 people attended over the course of three nights, and 9,521 came forward to make professions of faith to follow Jesus Christ as Savior and Lord. On Saturday evening, which was our youth outreach, most of them were under 30, and thousands flooded the backfield when I gave the invitation.

One was a scary-looking dude wearing a T-shirt that said "In Satan We Trust." He wept and prayed to God for forgiveness and new life. Afterward, he stood up, smiled a huge smile, stripped off his T-shirt and threw it away. "I don't need this anymore!" he shouted.

Years ago, a guy who made his living dealing drugs came forward at a crusade. The next day the man who had counseled him called to see how he was doing. "Great, I'm just mowing the grass," the former dealer told him.

"Oh, doing yard work?" the counselor asked.

"Sort of," said the ex-dealer. "I'm mowing down my field of marijuana plants!"

When I come to a city like Anaheim, newspaper reporters always press me to comment on political and moral issues. These are of course important, but when I'm in town for an event designed to reach people who are not yet believers, I don't want to cloud the gospel message by getting tagged with a political label. I don't come to a crusade to speak on hot-button issues like abortion, for example. Don't misunderstand: I'm completely pro-life. I easily could have been an abortion statistic, and I address this topic in my own church regularly. As a pastor, I try to equip my congregation to wrestle with a biblically informed worldview on any number of topics.

But in an evangelistic event, I want to reach out to *individuals*. I want to talk with real people who may be facing an unplanned pregnancy or who are gay or who have all kinds of challenges in their lives. Our Harvest team comes to show these people the love of God, His provision for them for eternity, and a community of people called the Church who can love them and welcome them in. We want them to know that they can change by God's power. I know that He changed me, and He can certainly change their lives, too.

Whenever we do crusades, we experience spiritual warfare. I come under spiritual attack; I get threats on my life and intimidation toward my family. There are spiritual hassles designed to wear down our whole team, as well as more malevolent powers of evil.

This is why we pray. We know we are in a battle for people's souls, and we arm ourselves with the Word of God, His Spirit and faith. We know that we are doing what God calls us to do, and that He is with us.

Satan's most powerful forms of attack on our crusades, however, don't come from dramatic external opposition. Satan doesn't have to send dark horses and chariots to assault our stadiums. All he has to do is pump up our pride, and then we're on our way to disaster. As the leader, I'm the most vulnerable to the pride attack. And one of the best weapons against it is one that came early on from—no surprise—Billy Graham.

Years ago, I was with Billy as one of his crusades drew to a close. The response was huge. After the final invitation, I walked with Billy and several of his associates through the narrow hallways underneath the stadium. Security men—necessary because of the threats he always received—surrounded Billy. We jumped into a four-door sedan, and police cars escorted us out of the stadium and into the street, their lights flashing.

It was like being with the president of the United States. I was watching Billy closely. How was he responding to the attention and celebrity of this kind of superstar status, not to mention the incredible spiritual import of so many conversions, so many lives transformed for eternity?

Others in the car were chatting about the high moments of the evening, but Billy was quiet, looking out the window. When we got to his hotel suite, he went into his room for a few minutes. The rest of us sat chatting. Before the crusade, a local pastor had brought in several bags full of barbecue sandwiches, but now they were cold. I wondered where we'd go out to eat, or if we'd just stay in and order room service.

Billy came out. To my surprise he had changed into a pair of cotton pajamas.

Evidently he had forgotten to pack his slippers; he was still wearing his dress shoes. He looked endearingly unstylish, and he was completely unselfconscious. I figured he just wanted to be comfortable.

We sat down. Someone got some paper napkins, and Billy passed out the cold barbecue sandwiches. We ate, laughed and talked about lots of different things. Ordinary things. Billy didn't even mention the crusade.

Sitting there with Billy Graham in his *Father Knows Best* PJs and his dress shoes, I saw one of the great antidotes to the pride that can come with the celebrity spotlight that shines on stadium evangelists. It's simple: Cultivate a keen sense of the ordinary.

Billy didn't relive the high points of the crusade like a quarterback exulting over the winning touchdown pass. No one ran the tapes so that we could clap Billy on the back and review the evening's moments of glory. He knew that there were hidden dangers in doing that, hooks that could snare his pride and tempt him to think that it was about him.

Billy knew it was all about God.

So I've tried to follow his example. After a crusade is the time to come back to my room, clean off my desk, play with my little granddaughter, catch up on email and eat a sandwich.

Nothing fancy.

It's time to move to the next thing, because if I linger on the crusade's great moments, it's easy to get hung up in a little piece of pride. And pride is never content with staying small.

There's another useful antidote to pride in my life these days. I never would have chosen it, but I should have expected it, since I didn't die young. It's called *aging*.

WHEN BOOMERS GET OLD

Yes, one of the fascinating cultural developments of the twenty-first century has been the phenomenon of people who so famously celebrated their youth with anthems like "My Generation" becoming members of AARP.

I guess every generation feels the same way—*How in the world can we be getting old?*—but for the former hippies and activists whose motto was "Never trust anyone over 30," it's a little ironic to be almost twice that age. We can't trust ourselves. Maybe we should update the chorus of the classic youth anthem by The Who from "Talkin' about my generation" to "Talkin' about my medication"!

We still feel young on the inside. But, as way too many comedians remind us, there are a few indications that things just aren't what they used to be.

Your back goes out more than you do.

Your mind makes commitments your body can't keep.

You find yourself actually singing along with the elevator music.

A while ago I had a classic senior moment. I had filled my tank at the gas pump. Perhaps I was distracted by the prices, because I drove away in a funk. Then I saw a man waving at my car. *I guess he recognizes me*, I thought. I waved back in a friendly fashion. Then a young woman was waving, trying to catch my eye as I continued to drive.

I smiled and nodded to her, thinking maybe I wasn't quite as old as I was feeling. Then a kid on a bike was waving his arms . . . and then I suddenly realized that I had careened away from the gas station pump with the nozzle still stuck in my tank. I looked in the rear view mirror and there it was, bumping along, still inserted in my car, following me like a black python down the street.

I died inside. *Maybe I should just keep going*, I thought. *Like to Mexico.*

But conscience prevailed, and I went back to the gas station, absolutely humiliated.

"Don't worry about it," the gas station attendant said reassuringly as I gave him his rubbery python back. "The nozzles and hoses are designed to break away from the pump. No big deal. Older people do it all the time."

"Oh, and . . ." he added, "that'll be $125."

I would have paid just about anything to get out of there. The only consolation was to discover that this happened quite frequently (at least among people of my generation).

One of the other discouraging things with the passing of time is the advance of my waistline and the retreat of my hair. I know far too many fat pastors, and I have fought the battle of the bulge for years. It's easy to gain weight in ministry. There are far too many potluck dinners, lunch meetings at restaurants, Bible studies over coffee and dessert, and prayer breakfasts.

Many fellow pastors have just given up, but I keep trying because of my wife's gentle encouragement and vigilant portion control. When we're in a restaurant, she orders one nice little entrée for both of us, and then she eats half of it.

Sadly, right around the same time I started gaining unwanted weight, I found that I was losing much-wanted hair. I first discovered this when I knew it was raining before anyone else. My wife, who has enough hair for three people, would say, "I don't feel a drop!" and I'd say (sweetly of course), "That's because you have to wait for the rain to hit the skin on your hands or face. But we bald guys have skin right on top, and we feel the rain right away." Bald guys are always the first to know when it's raining.

My hair started departing for destinations unknown when I was in my late 20s. By my mid-30s, it was almost gone. Since this coincided with the end of the '80s, a decade not known for good taste—spandex, shoulder pads and disco couture were among its fashion contributions— I began to perfect what is known in balding circles as the "combover." (Actually, Cathe and I called it "the flap," because that's what it did in a strong wind.)

The idea in this misguided enterprise is to grow your hair extra long on one side of your head and pull it over the top to the other side, attaching it firmly with a lot of hairspray.

I elevated this to an art form.

During my flap period I was at a Billy Graham Crusade in Portland, Oregon. A sudden downpour commenced, and unfortunately, there was no cover for those of us sitting on the platform in the huge open-air arena. I was sitting next to Cliff Barrows, Billy's long-time friend and song leader, and someone took a photo of us that night.

The rain was coming down in sheets. Cliff's suit, like mine, was a disaster, and his hair was soaking wet and plastered to his head. But in the photo, preserved for the ages, my hair seems to be defying all known natural laws of thermodynamics: It was so plastered with bullet-proof, rain-proof hairspray that my flap was absolutely in place. It looks like the immovable horns of a Southeast Asian water buffalo.

Sadly, my hair habits were not the exception. Much to the delight of comedians everywhere, pastors and evangelists seem to be a key market for toupees. Years ago if you attended a National Religious Broadcasters' convention, you would see hundreds of hairpieces, in addition to flaps, combovers, poofs, and hair treatments as yet un-named. It seemed like some of us weren't sure if we were preachers or Elvis impersonators.

My buddy Dennis Agajanian is an incredible guitar picker who brings audiences to their feet at our Harvest Crusades. He's a sight worth seeing: six-foot-four, with black shirts, boots, jeans, a belt with a buckle the size of a dinner plate and an enormous cowboy hat. Years ago, Dennis told me about a Christian friend who had made a really realistic-looking hairpiece for him. The friend was willing to make one for me as well, and the price was right: It was free!

Dennis modeled his new rug for me, and when I stood on a ladder and examined the top of his head, I had to admit it wasn't bad at all.

A couple of months went by, and when my hairpiece finally arrived, it was a work of follicle art. But when I put it on, it just didn't look right. My lovely wife, who is blessed with incredible hair, did not care for the piece at all. (It's easy for her to say. I could take what's left over from her brush after one day and have a revival on my head.) Although I really never intended to wear it, I felt bad about all the excellent work that had gone into creating the piece. So I ventured out with it on . . . and the first strong wind terrified me. My rug almost went airborne.

As the wind flipped up the back of the piece, you could read the inscription its creator had sewn inside: *For Pastor Greg Laurie. Praise the Lord!* I did want to praise the Lord, but I had seen a photo of it on my head, and it looked like a bird's nest. Around that time I read that one of my favorite authors, Peggy Noonan, described a hairpiece as "a lie on your head." That made sense to me, and I didn't want to be proclaiming the truth while wearing a lie. So I stowed my toupee in my closet.

Our house had been built not long before that in a tract that had formerly been a big meadow, and we had a little problem with field mice when the weather turned cold. They popped up in our closets and crawl spaces. And so when my hairpiece mysteriously disappeared, I could only assume that a mouse had dragged it away in the night, thinking it was a long-lost relative. My name was labeled inside, of course, so every now and then I comb through eBay expecting to see my missing piece for sale: a relic from the '80s that belonged to a genuine relic from the 1950s.

I'm told that the French have a proverb that says, "Forty is the old age of youth and fifty is the young of old age." That means I am now officially a young old person. And with that, I'm seeing that the passing years will bring increasing limitations. You lose physical abilities; you lose friends and loved ones. Your hair falls out and you get old-man spotted hands.

Someone has calibrated the years of one's life to the hours of the day. If you are 15, the time is 10:25 A.M. If you are 20, it's 11:34; 30, it's 1:51 P.M. If you are 40 years old, your time is 4:08; at 50, it's 6:25; and so on.

So for me, the time is about 7:30 P.M.—which is sad, because I've been going to bed by about 9:30 these days.

Greg Laurie
Corona del Mar High School Yearbook photo
circa 1960s

The McDaniel family, including Daddy Charles and Mama Stella (center, bottom row), Aunt Willie (second from left, bottom row), and Greg's mother, Charlene (second from right, bottom row).

Greg in his Military School uniform at age 11.

Charlene at Christmas, circa early 1960s.

Greg and Charlene, sometime in the 1950s.

Greg, age 6, hanging out with his brother Doug.

Greg on the beach in Newport, California, early 1960s.

Greg and a friend at Christmas, late 1950s.

Greg at the San Diego Zoo, late 1950s.

DEAR SIRS...

I AM WRITING IN REGARD TO YOUR NEW PUBLICATON

 " WHICH

I THINK IS A SUPERIOR SURFING PUBLICATION AND I WAS WONDERING IF YOU WOULD LIKE TO EMPLOY A CARTOONIST. I COULD SUBMIT GAGS OR SEND A WHOLE COMIC STRIP, OR COMIC STORYS... HERE IS A PICTURE OF ONE OF MY LATEST "SURFING" CHARACTERS." HE IS

"CLYDE DABUM" THIS GUY'S A TYPICAL SURFING-BUM. I HAVE ENCLOSED A CARTOON FEATURING THIS SURFIN BUM. MY OTHER CAST OF CHARACTERS INCLUDE "GOOBERS McGOOBERS", HIS TALKING DOG "HERMAN" "SEMOUR DOWINITLE", AND HIS FOLKS...
THESE TWO CHARACTERS COULD BE FEATURED IN SURFING STORIES BY THE DOZEN.

G.L.

G.L.

SO, ENCLOSED IS "CLYDE DABUM IN HOLLYWOOD OR BUST," "THE INQUIZITIVE YOUNG-MAN", "AND CARTOON REVIEW OF GOOBERS AND THE GANG. SO THE DESISIAN IS YOURS. IF YOU WISH ME TO SEND YOU A BATCH OF ONE-PANEL SURFING CARTOONS I WILL DO SO ... THANX

P.S. PLEASE RETURN CARTOONS IF YOU DO NOT WISH TO PUBLISH THEM.

GREG LAURIE
1810, WEST OCEAN PT. # C
NEWPORT BEACH, CALIF.
92660

Greg's application for a job as a cartoonist at *Surf* magazine, mid-1960s.

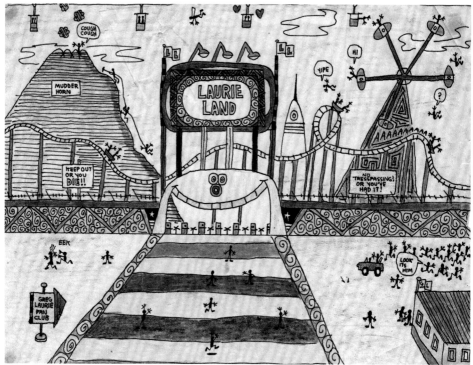

Greg's attempt at humor with Laurie Land.

Greg's cartoon family, 1969. Greg retreated into his private world of cartoons, where things were happier and families were intact.

Work day at Greg's new church, early 1970s.

Greg makes a new friend, early 1970s.

Cathe when Greg first met her, age 15, early 1970s.

Greg leading worship, early 1970s.

Greg's adopted father, Oscar Felix Laurie. Greg had the honor of baptizing Oscar after his conversion in the early 1980s.

Chuck Smith helps Greg reach the berries in Austria, late 1980s.

Greg leads prayer at a Billy Graham Crusade in 1985.

Senator Elizabeth Dole, Bob Shank, Greg Laurie and Chuck Smith at a Harvest Crusade in the late 1990s.

Larry King interviewing Rod Parsley and Greg on *Larry King Live* (photo by Mark Ferjulian).

Greg with James Dobson at the White House, 2004.

Greg with Chuck Norris.

Jonathan, Cathe, Greg, Brittany, Stella and Christopher Laurie in New York City, 2007.

Cathe, Jonathan, Christopher and Greg in 2006.

Greg riding his Harley-Davidson.

Greg and Cathe have been married for 34 years.

Though the stadium is usually packed for a Harvest Crusade, people often say that they feel as if Greg is speaking to them one-on-one.

Jane and Franklin Graham, Greg, President George H. W. Bush and Mrs. Bush, Cathe and President Jimmy Carter, at the dedication of the Billy Graham Library, 2007.

Greg presents a bithday present to Billy Graham, 2007.

Greg still hangs out in Newport, 2006.

Greg working on his next book . . .

OSCAR COMES HOME

Oscar Laurie adopted me and gave me his name on September 20, 1959. I was six years old, and Oscar gave me my first taste of what a loving father could be. When my mom and I lived with him in New Jersey, life was different. I didn't have to wait up at night for my mother to come in. I could just be a kid, playing with toy cars on the floor, ice skating on the frozen lakes, and raking up big piles of autumn leaves and jumping into them.

But as I've said, after a few years, that peaceful season came to an abrupt end when my mom pulled me out of school and to a new life in Hawaii with an abusive drunk named Eddie.

After I came to know Jesus and had been pastoring at Harvest for about five years, I wanted to reconnect with Oscar. My mother had no contact with him, and wouldn't have approved if I told her I was trying to find him. But with the help of a church friend who worked for a bar association, I was able to track Oscar down.

I called his law office number and an assistant answered the phone.

"I'd like to speak with Oscar Laurie, please," I said.

"May I tell him who's calling?" she asked.

"Yes, it's Greg," I said. "Greg *Laurie*."

"How do you spell your last name?" she asked.

"The same way he spells his last name," I said. "This is his son!"

There was a moment of awkward silence.

"I'll get this message to him right away, Mr. Laurie!"

In a moment, Oscar Laurie picked up the phone. His voice shook with excitement. I had been afraid he wouldn't be pleased by my intrusion . . . but Oscar said he was thrilled to hear from me.

I told Oscar that I was coming to New York soon for a speaking engagement, and that I wanted to meet him for lunch, if possible. I was trying to keep it as light and easy for him as I could. I thought the father-son dynamic was most likely a thing of the distant past.

"No!" he said. "You must come and stay at our house!"

Oscar had remarried several years after my mom left him. He had a family. I didn't want to impose, but he insisted, and so after I preached at an outreach in Manhattan, I took the train to his New Jersey town. As we pulled into the Redbank station, my heart was thumping. I grabbed my wife's hand and climbed off the train and onto the platform. And there, in the distance, I saw Oscar coming toward me.

He had a broad smile on his face. He was older, of course, but his walk and his attitude were just as I remembered.

Suddenly I was a little boy again. Before I could catch myself, I shouted, "Dad!" We ran to each other and embraced in an enormous hug.

Cathe and I spent three nights visiting with Oscar and his wife, Barbara. She fed us ziti with sausage and peppers from their garden, creamy cannelloni, and rich coffee. I considered staying for a month.

Oscar told me that he'd had a major heart attack a few months earlier. He had almost died, but was doing much better. As we sipped coffee after dinner, Barbara said, "Greg, tell us how you became a pastor."

I shared my story of coming to Christ, and how God had led me to preach and evangelize. Barbara nodded, smiled and asked leading questions. Oscar, however, reminded me a little bit of the biblical character Nicodemus. He was a moral man, educated, full of integrity. But he didn't know Jesus in a personal way. He hadn't been born again. He sat at the other end of the table, taking it all in quietly, like a judge listening to an attorney present his case.

I thought, *This is not going well.*

At the end of the evening, Oscar finally said something. "Well, Greg, do you want to go walking with me in the morning?" He explained that his doctor had told him he had to get daily exercise because of his heart condition.

"Sure," I said. "What time?"

"I'll knock on your door at 6," he said.

I would have gotten up at 3 for the opportunity to walk with my dad.

The next morning, it was still dark when Oscar rapped on my door. "Greg, wake up!" I felt like a little boy again. Dad was getting me up for school.

We headed toward the walking paths in the park. "Greg," Oscar said, "I listened very carefully to what you said last night." Suddenly I was wide awake. "I thought about it," he continued in his methodical way, "and I want to become a Christian. Right now."

Even though Cathe and I had prayed for this exact moment, I could not believe it was actually happening. I had thought he was just being polite when he listened to my story the night before, and now I thought he may have misunderstood me. So I went over the gospel again.

"Yes," said Oscar. "I want Jesus Christ to come into my life!"

Could it be? Could something good be coming out the mess I had gone through as a child?

"We should pray," I said excitedly.

"Okay," he said.

He got down on his knees, right there in the park. I dropped to the ground next to him, put my arm around his shoulders, and he prayed for God to forgive his sins and enter his life. Tears flowed down his cheeks.

As soon as the prayer was completed, Oscar said, "I know the Lord has come into my heart. Let's pray for my heart, that God would heal my cardiac condition. He can do it." We prayed about Oscar's heart, and then we got up. "I think God has healed me," he said. "Let's go tell my doctor."

"Now wait a minute, Dad," I said. "We know Christ has come into your life, but we don't know if He has healed your heart condition!"

"Well, I think He has," Oscar said steadfastly.

We walked straight to his Jewish doctor's office, which was (fortunately) nearby.

"I just got saved," Oscar told him. "Christ is in my life and I'm healed!"

I had a smile on my face, not sure what to think of my father's zeal. I knew he'd been converted; I just wasn't sure that his physical heart had been healed.

The doctor's eyebrows shot up.

"This is my son Greg," Oscar went on. "He's the pastor of a big church in Southern California."

Ah, I could see the doctor thinking. *One of those California nutcases!*

But out loud he said, "Now, Oscar, we'll need to run some tests before we know if anything has changed regarding your heart."

Oscar was adamant, though. Jesus had come into his life, and he knew his heart was better.

It was hard for me to leave New Jersey and return to California. Before I left, I found a strong, Bible-teaching church for my dad and his wife to attend, and bought him a modern translation of the Old and New Testaments.

"Just start reading the Bible," I told him. "I'll be back!"

Three weeks later, I returned. I was afraid he might have lost his fervor. We sat down together and I read him a verse from the New Testament.

"Oh, yes," he said. "That's from the apostle Paul in Ephesians, right?"

"That's right," I said, surprised.

Oscar had read the entire Bible in the three weeks I'd been gone. He was studying it, digesting it, chewing on it during his morning walks and thinking about it in his bed at night. And it was changing his life.

Oscar eventually became an elder in his church. His wife and two other sons became believers. He got involved with the Gideons, helping to distribute Bibles across the U.S. and around the world.

And his heart *was* healed. He'd had a congenital condition all his life that mysteriously disappeared, according to his doctor. Oscar had been an upstanding, moral man, but once he met Jesus and was born again, he was irrepressible, bubbling over like a fountain full of joy and service to God. He lived 14 more incredibly fruitful years.

Two years after Oscar came to faith, he wrote me a letter about his changed perspective:

Dearest Son—

You may remember that you once told me that as you read and re-read certain passages of the Bible, you discovered meanings that you had not previously observed. I thought about that the other night when I had finished reading the Gospel according to St. John.

I reflected for a while and I thought about how the Lord really does work according to His will. I thought about how angry I was about the end of my marriage to your mother and how I rejected the Lord at that time. Yet the Lord used that whole disaster in my life to chasten me and to ultimately turn my life around through you.

I prayed to the Lord in thanksgiving for you, and for how God brought us together again, resulting in me being born again and placing my life in the hands of the Lord and accepting Jesus as my Lord and Savior.

—Dad

I will cherish that letter as long as I live. There, in black and white, it shows me that God is faithful to do far beyond what I could ever hope. God used disasters for good—not only in my life, but in Oscar's as well.

On December 26, 1994, Oscar went to be with the Lord. I miss him. But because of God's grace, I will see him again one day . . . the man who adopted me and showed me the love of an earthly father so that I could one day recognize the love of my heavenly Father.

3 0

PRODIGAL SURPRISES

The Bible says that believers are to "Be on duty at all times," ready for any opportunity to tell someone about Jesus (see 1 Pet. 3:15).

Any opportunity.

Such a moment came for me when I was in the men's room, of all places, in a department store in Riverside.

I went into a stall and was minding my own business, so to speak. I heard a guy come in and settle into the stall next to me. I didn't think much of it until I heard him clear his throat. It was a communication cough, not a throat-clearing cough.

"Hey," he whispered.

I didn't know where to look. I said nothing.

He coughed again. "Were you supposed to meet me here?"

What on earth is this? I thought. I really did not want to communicate with this stranger. "No!" I replied firmly.

A moment of silence passed.

"Uh, do you have something for me?" he asked.

My curiosity got the best of me in spite of the weirdness of the situation.

"What is it you're looking for, exactly?" I asked.

"I was going to buy some drugs," he replied.

His naiveté surprised me. For all he knew, I could be a police officer, not the dealer he assumed was waiting for him.

"Well, I don't have any drugs," I said. "But I've got something better."

"What?" the guy asked. Now *he* was curious.

"A personal relationship with God, through Jesus Christ," I replied.

I went on to tell my unseen companion how I had experimented with drugs for a time, that it was a dead-end street, and that God had a better plan for his life.

"Oh, I tried that," he sighed. "I even went to church."

"What church?" I asked.

"Right here in Riverside," he went on. "That huge church. Harvest Christian Fellowship."

I choked. "Do you know who I am?" I asked.

"No, of course not," he said.

"I'm Greg Laurie, the *pastor* of Harvest Christian Fellowship!"

There was silence from the other stall. "Oh, my God," he finally muttered.

I laughed, "Buddy, God must sure love you a lot to send your pastor right to you when you're in the restroom trying to make a drug buy!"

I felt that the usefulness of our setting had run its course, so I told my prodigal friend that I'd meet him outside the bathroom in the men's department. I stood by the sock display, and he was easy to spot. He was the guilty-looking guy.

My heart went out to him. We talked for a while, and then he decided he wanted to pray and get right with God. We did that, right by the socks, right by the bathroom.

Usually my evangelism isn't in a confined one-on-one setting like a bathroom stall. At our crusades, I get to tell thousands of people at one time about the love of God. It's astonishing. Yet one of the hardest things over the years was to see thousands of people come to Christ in our crusades, in our church and through various media outlets, and yet have my own mother continue in her state of unbelief.

Or so I thought.

When I first became a Christian, I blasted my mom with both barrels of my newly acquired gospel shotgun. But as time passed and I began to mature in my faith, I realized this was the wrong approach.

My mom knew—or thought she knew—the gospel. She had heard it since her youth, going back to her childhood days at the Baptist church in Friendship, Arkansas. But somewhere along the way, she had gotten the idea that faith was all about rules and regulations. She missed the Good News about grace, and she got to the point where she couldn't even hear it because she was so turned off by her false understanding of the gospel. To her, Christianity had to do with dressing a certain way—no pants—and sitting in long, dull church services.

She felt that if she became a Christian, she'd never have any fun.

So she ran away from it all and eloped at age 17, thinking that her sailor would sweep her away to the bright lights and good times of the big city. Then she traded her husband in for a new one, then another, and on it went as she partied with the beautiful people in Newport and Waikiki Beach.

One night my mother, Charlene, had followed her usual nightly routine of working at her restaurant until it closed, then sitting at the bar for an hour or two. Cigarette in hand, she stumbled into her pale-yellow 1965 Mustang. She pulled out onto a major boulevard in Newport Beach, drove right over the center divider, and hit an oncoming car head-on.

It was a miracle that neither the other driver nor my mother was killed. My mom was thrown against the steering wheel with such force that most of her teeth were knocked out. (No air bags on those '60s cars.) Her beautiful face was smashed; blood was everywhere. In the drunken disaster of a moment, the identity she'd had all her life—the gorgeous Marilyn Monroe look-alike who stopped traffic—was crumpled and thrown away into the night, gone forever.

Though her lovely face was now swollen and marred, she recovered physically from her accident. And she began to slowly soften to spiritual things. I first started noticing it when we had prayer before meals. Over the years, Cathe and I had always offered a short prayer of thanks whenever we dined out with my mom. She didn't protest it, and I always felt that it was a small act of courtesy on her part to allow us our prayer, even if she didn't see the need for it.

But one evening when we were out with Mom and her husband, Bill, I guess we were ravenous or distracted or something. After our food arrived, Cathe and I did not pause to give thanks, but dug into our plates like starving pagans. Then I noticed that my mother was not eating . . . and I realized that she was waiting for us to say grace! I apologized, we prayed, and I went back to my meal at a much slower rate, but it dawned on me that this was perhaps a small, hopeful sign of spiritual interest on my mother's part.

But she was by no means ready for any big discussions about theology, epistemology, salvation, sanctification, predestination, or any of the other -ations or -ologies. Mom always liked things at a nice, surface level. She loved tabloids, *The National Enquirer*, *People* magazine, celebrity gossip and the latest of who's-doing-what-with-whom. I guess if she could no longer live the high life, she wanted to read all about it. It seemed to me that she was always hungry for celebrity.

It didn't seem to matter to her just what a person was famous for, as long as he or she was famous. Charlene had longed for applause, notoriety and attention all her life. She was intrigued by the spotlight. As Harvest grew, if I happened to meet famous people, or if there was a newspaper article about a crusade, or if I was interviewed on television, *then* my mom was interested. She loved when I was in the news. She saved newspaper clippings and told my aunts how proud she was . . . though she never mentioned that to me.

But if conversation turned to weightier matters—like what I might *say* about the gospel when I was in the spotlight—then you could be sure my mom would withdraw, like a snail coming in contact with a saltshaker. Charlene liked to keep it light.

When I told her the story of how her former husband, Oscar, had come to Christ, she listened politely. "That's nice," she said.

I pressed her on her own spiritual state, and she gave me her standard reply: "I don't want to talk about it!"

One night she called me. It was late, and she'd been drinking.

"Gerger!" she said. Her nickname for me had come as a result of her drunkenly slurring my name and apparently liking the result. She called me that for years. I hated it.

"If I went forward at one of your services to follow Jesus," she continued, "would you have the choir sing 'Just as I Am'?"

My jaw dropped. I motioned to Cathe, awakened by the ringing phone, to pray.

"Mother," I said, "if you come forward to commit your life to Jesus, I will have the choir sing absolutely anything you want!"

She'd been drinking and remembering her childhood in the Baptist church. Experience told me she would not remember our conversation the next morning, but I was hopeful anyway. I called her the next day and went over our whole exchange from the night before.

"Greg!" she said sternly. "I *don't* want to talk about it!"

Our dance around the gospel went on for years. I learned I couldn't force my mom to come to Jesus—or I would have. I would have been more than happy to ask Jesus into her heart. But it just doesn't work that way.

As she got older, she got weaker. Her lifestyle had taken its toll; her kidneys were failing and she had to have dialysis three times a week.

One day I felt God pulling me to talk with my mom about her spiritual state. I asked Cathe to pray.

I knocked on my mother's door, and no one else was with her. "We need to have a talk about where you are spiritually," I said.

My mom probably started having flashbacks to her childhood and thought I was going to cut up her trousers and throw them into the fire.

"I do not want to have this discussion!" she shot back.

But I was her son, and I could be stubborn too. "No," I said. "We *are* going to have this discussion!"

First I asked her about my father. My actual, biological father. For years I'd known it wasn't the man listed on my birth certificate. But it was time to know whose DNA I carried within me, besides my mother's stubborn genes.

"Your real father's name is Barney," she told me.

I was so stunned that she was finally admitting his identity that my first reaction was on the most superficial level possible.

"Barney?" I sputtered. The only Barney I could think of was Barney Fife, Andy Griffith's deputy . . . and then there was Barney Rubble, Fred Flintstone's neighbor. (Thankfully, this was before the era of Barney the purple dinosaur.)

This is not to denigrate the name Barney. There are many wonderful Barneys in the world.

"Where was he from?" I asked.

"Canada," she said. "He was a good dancer."

My father: Barney, the Canadian dancer.

This conversation about my birth dad was so surreal that I quickly returned to the most important issue at hand: What was going on with my mom spiritually?

It was like navigating a treacherous reef. She gave no encouraging signs. She was clearly uncomfortable. Yet for once she was listening and not fighting me.

Suddenly I saw my mom in a new light: not as the hard-drinking party animal, but as the once-young girl who had grown up in a stifling home without affirmation or affection, who had tried to fill her need for love by running away and looking for it in all the wrong places. I had always thought of her as a tough, cynical nonbeliever. Now I saw her as a prodigal . . . someone who had run away from the heavenly Father's love and might not quite know how to find her way back home.

"Mother," I asked her. "Do you consider yourself a Christian?"

"Yes, I do!" she replied almost indignantly.

Are you kidding me? I thought, but out loud I said, "Have you put your faith in Jesus Christ as your Savior and Lord?"

"Yes!" she said again.

This is not the answer I expected, and for once this preacher was at a loss for words.

Then I blurted out, "Well, if you're a Christian, why don't you go to church and spend time with other believers?"

I thought she would say because they didn't serve alcohol in church, but to my shock she had no snappy comeback.

It was close to Christmas, and we were having a special event at our church with country music celebrity Randy Travis. It was right up her alley, so I invited her. Obviously we had asked her to come to our church many, many times over the years. But now something was different . . . and not only did she agree to come to the service, she actually showed up.

Even in her older years, she fixed herself up to look as pretty as she could. Her hair was still blonde, and she always wore bright, festive colors with matching accessories. But she was quite ill that day, and had already thrown up several times. We set things up so that she could watch the service on a sofa in my office, via a live television feed.

For Christmas, I bought my mom a television with a built-in DVD player because she could never figure out how to operate her separate DVD system. I set up the combo in her living room and brought over DVDs of a few of Billy Graham's greatest sermons, as well as disks of Chuck Smith preaching, and even a few of my own. I felt like she was actually open to bringing the gospel onto her turf; she had crossed immeasurable barriers by coming to the service at our church. As Cathe and I prayed hopefully, I began dreaming that my mom would get stronger both spiritually and physically, and that we'd have many sweet, fruitful years of an entirely new relationship.

Maybe I could give my mom some kind of job at our church, I thought. *People would welcome her warmly, and she could be part of a healthy working environment. We could eat lunch together and make up for all those years that wafted away in an alcoholic haze. We lost so much time in the past . . . but God could redeem those years.*

Because my mom's health seemed to be improving, Cathe and I felt comfortable leaving town for a week right after Christmas. We were traveling with friends who owned a beautiful yacht, and they had invited us to be their guests, along with another couple. There were six of us happily sailing around in the Caribbean, surrounded by emerald seas.

On New Year's Eve, we spent the day walking along on deserted white-sand beaches, singing hymns as loud as we could. That evening we sat on the rolling deck and watched the sun set on the violet horizon. In the golden end of the old year, we reflected on God's great faithfulness. We dreamed a little about our hopes for the New Year. We talked a little bit about resolutions. Mine was to be kinder to people. We went to bed, rocking in the peaceful darkness of new beginnings.

Early on New Year's morning, we got a phone call from Carol, my wonderful assistant. I was excited that she was calling: I'd left my computer on the plane to our lovely destination, and I assumed that Carol, in her usual efficient way, had tracked it down.

Our phone connection was weak, but it sounded like Carol was weeping. "Greg!" she said, her voice breaking. "I am so sorry to have to tell you this, but it's your mother . . ."

My heart constricted. "What?" I asked.

"Greg, your mom died last night," Carol said. "I am so sorry!"

I fell down on the deck. I cried like I had never cried in my life, years of emotions pouring out of me in a flood of pain. I wept for my mom, that she had never lived the free, bold life she could have had in a relationship with God. I wept for myself, that I had lost the only mother I'd ever known. I wept because I was filled with guilt: I should have been by her side. In my tears that day, I didn't weep because of the way I'd felt most of my life: that Charlene had been a poor mother. I wept because I was a poor son.

Tears coursed down my face as I thought in a new way about the old story of the prodigal. I saw Charlene, having wasted her life in the pigsties of this world, coming back to the heavenly Father who had loved her and given her life. I could imagine Him, His arms outstretched, running to meet her at heaven's bright gate. I could imagine friends welcoming her to come farther up and farther in to the glorious feast in heaven, the golden party in the spotlight that my mom had been searching for all her life.

The prodigal had finally come home.

It was tragic, though, in the sense of her earthly years; she had wasted so many of them, chasing after the wind. But fortunately, in my mom's restless life, God had the last word: *Forgiven*.

DNA AND OTHER LOOSE ENDS

After Oscar Laurie's passing in 1994 and my mother's death in 2000, I felt like I still had a piece of unfinished business. Like many children who become adults without having met their birth fathers, I had a dream in the back of my mind of what he would be like.

I dreamed he'd be someone I could look up to, someone I could laugh with, someone in whom I could see my heritage, my habits and even my hair. Though my renewed adult relationship with Oscar Laurie had been an incredible blessing, I still had a small hole inside. Or maybe I was just plain curious. For all I knew, Barney Bingham (as I'll call him) could be the secret heir to a foreign throne, a Nobel Prize winner, or perhaps even a Christian.

But I kind of doubted it.

My experiences with my mother had taught me to lower my expectations. I thought of how I had sought out her former abusive husband, Eddie, and shared the gospel with him, with high hopes—and what a dismal failure that had been.

It happened after Oscar had come to faith, so maybe I thought that I was on a roll and that something similar could happen with Eddie. I tracked him down.

His opulent home was long gone. Cathe and I walked from the bright sunshine and brilliant blue skies of Hawaii into Eddie's dark, cramped apartment. The furniture was worn and dingy. The shades were drawn. Eddie sat in a chair, the shrapnel-filled leg that had plagued him since World War II propped in front of him. He'd refused to let doctors amputate it and had sought to ease his pain with alcohol for years. Now he was a broken old man.

My heart went out to him.

I enthusiastically shared my story of how I had come to faith, and how Jesus could touch his life, too. Eddie listened, but said nothing. I told him I was speaking at some meetings nearby and that I'd be happy to pick him up so that he could come. He was not interested.

I asked if he had any desire to believe in Jesus. He shook his head. *No.*

As far as I ever knew, Eddie wasn't open to the gospel, and I had no assurance that my birth father, Barney, would be interested either. But then I thought of Oscar again and how God had so wonderfully prepared him to hear the gospel, and how he had opened his heart to Jesus after just one extended conversation.

I was mulling these things over when one day, all of the sudden, I picked up the phone and called Karen Johnson, the wife of my friend Pastor Jeff Johnson. She has helped thousands of Christian families adopt unwanted babies. She has access to old birth records and other information that can be hard to locate and had told me to call her if I ever needed help finding my biological father.

I told Karen the vital statistics I knew about Barney. Let's see: Canadian, sailor, stationed in Long Beach for at least one night in March 1952. Reddish-blond hair. It wasn't much to go on.

Half an hour later the phone rang. Karen had found my Barney.

She had actually spoken with Barney's wife on the phone, and it was clear we had the right man. His wife said she wasn't surprised by the call; Barney had been a chronic ladies' man in his day. One other thing, she added: Barney had been quite a dancer. I hadn't mentioned that detail to Karen, but it was one of the few things my mother had emphasized about him.

Barney was living on the big island of Hawaii, of all places.

Hawaii again. It had such powerful, mixed memories for me. I remembered peaceful beaches, soft breezes, big blue waves and the freedom of going to school barefooted. I remembered the salt-rot smell of Eddie's bar, The Lava Lounge, the gurgle of drinks being poured, the crash of broken glass and the sight of Eddie standing over my bleeding mother on the floor. It was in Hawaii that I knew the pain of losing Oscar Laurie, the fear of Eddie, the confusion of pre-adolescence and the loneliness of not knowing where I fit.

Now I would return to the islands, but this time to meet the dancing Canadian man who had swept sunny Charlene right off her feet in Long Beach in 1952. I wondered what it had been like for them. There they were, in some bar. Had they taken the time to know one another, to talk, to share thoughts, dreams and hopes? Or did they just see each other, make a connection, down a few drinks and fall into bed?

Whatever the case, I was the result. I didn't want to romanticize the situation to make it more palatable. I just wanted the truth, and maybe this visit with Barney would somehow shed light on the mystery of it all.

I would have loved to have been born as the eagerly awaited child of stable parents, then dedicated to God as a bouncing baby in the church community—loved, welcomed and nurtured. Instead, I was the illegitimate result of a one-night stand. Back in the 1950s, being born "out of wedlock" was scandalous, so my mother had covered up my origins by marrying another man quite quickly. Though his name was on my birth certificate, it was a lie.

I was just a baby, a little lost boy, and my beginnings were shrouded in lies like a spider web, sticky strands of shame I could not escape. My mother had waited almost 50 years to tell me the truth about my birth father. I didn't know how to think of him. Was he just my biological heir, supplier of half my gene pool, or was there some great emotional linkage here that would fill in the missing pieces in my story?

I thought about my sons and my granddaughter. If there had been no Barney and Charlene, there would be no Greg. No Christopher and Jonathan. No granddaughter Stella.

I knew that contacting Barney would change my life in some way. I had just come through the trauma of my mom dying, and I did not feel I needed a new crisis to deal with at the moment.

I stared at the phone. It just seemed like it was time for me to see my birth father. Cathe had wisely pointed out that we might discover genetic issues that would be important for our children and their children. I agreed; I also felt that this was a chapter of my life that had to be read. But I certainly would have preferred just leaving it out and rewriting the whole story.

I picked up the phone and punched the newly acquired numbers that would connect me to my actual father. Karen had told me that Barney's wife would answer the phone; that made it easier.

So did her kindness regarding my quest. She invited us to come to their home. "But you'd better come soon," she said. *Soon.* Barney was in his 80s now, and he had the beginnings of Alzheimer's.

Cathe and I landed at the airport in Kona. The warm tradewinds blew over us, but I was full of cold dread as we began our pilgrimage to my biological father's house. He lived in a remote area, and we drove for hours. I had a knot in my stomach as Cathe and I talked with each other and prayed about this strange meeting.

We finally found the road. We pulled onto a long and winding driveway. Barney's home was a little place with rock work and landscaping that he must have done in years gone by. I began to doubt that he was a Nobel Prize winner or the secret heir to a foreign throne.

Barney's wife opened the door, and I caught my first glimpse of him. He was sitting in an old fabric chair, legs stretched out, staring at the television. His gray hair was combed straight back, but I could see a few wisps that had once been reddish-blond.

He stared blankly at us. "Hello, how are you?" he asked mechanically. I might as well have been selling door-to-door magazine subscriptions. There was no curiosity, no cosmic recognition, nothing.

Meanwhile his wife kept chatting away.

Actually, she told us more about the man she had been married to before Barney than about Barney. She and Cathe kept a conversation going while I kept stealing glances at him.

It's a mistake, I thought. *Why did I even come here?*

His wife told us that Barney had appeared in bit parts on the '60s TV series *Hawaii Five-O*. Now that was bizarre: I had loved that show and watched it often even after my mother and I fled Eddie and Hawaii. I wondered if I had ever seen any of the episodes in which Barney was on screen. I would have been looking at my own flesh and blood, through the prism of the fantasy world of television.

I snapped out of my daze and entered into the conversation, telling Barney about my journey in life, how I'd become a Christian and a pastor/evangelist. I told him how I'd emerged from my lost beginnings to a lifestyle and a family that was so different than how I had grown up. I told him about the love of God, just as I had Oscar, Eddie and the other men my mom had been involved with. (Reaching out to my mom's old flames was becoming a full-time ministry.)

But Barney did not seem to care. We showed him an old photo of my mom, at the age she would have been when they met for drinks that night in Long Beach. Barney shook his head. He didn't recognize her.

He can't be my biological father, I thought . . . but down deep, I realized he probably was. We had similar height, build and coloring. His wife showed us photographs of Barney when he was younger, and his strawberry-blond hair was just like mine.

Then Cathe noted the clincher: Barney had an unusual physical trait. The middle finger on his right hand curved toward the left; the middle finger on his left hand curved toward the right. The rest of his fingers were straight.

My hands were absolutely identical.

I was crestfallen. There had to be a happier ending than this.

We exchanged a few more pleasantries, and left Barney and his wife with a couple of books I had written . . . but neither of them seemed to care very much.

During the long ride back to Kona, Cathe and I didn't talk a lot. I wished I'd never made the trip. It was so hollow, so full of nothing. *Well, I thought in frustration, now I can "get on with my life," as they say.* There were no more fathers to search for. No more questions about whether or not my biological father was alive or where he lived. His name was Barney, he lived in Hawaii, and he did not know me or care about me. In some ways it was worse than if he'd been dead . . . at least then I could have cherished dreams about what things could have been like.

I realized then that I was still carrying around images in my head, pictures of Barney somehow being a dad to me. I guess I'd had subconscious fantasies of us spending time together when he'd take me fishing or teach me how to throw a baseball, or show me how to tie my tie properly or to change the oil in my car. I thought of all the little things I never learned how to do growing up because I'd never had a dad. And now I never would.

Well, I thought in my cynical way, *it could have been worse. Barney could be in prison, a serial killer. Or he could be the head of a telemarketing firm.*

DISAPPOINTMENT WITH GOD?

What was I going to do with my lost boy story, now that I had found Barney? I realized that how I dealt with this disappointment really didn't have so much to do with how I viewed my birth father. It had everything to do with how I viewed God.

I looked back over my growing-up years: the fear-filled nights, military school, chaos, constant moves to another new relationship for my mom and another new school for me, then break-ups, divorce, another move. My aunt tells me that when I was a toddler, I'd cry when my mom would leave. "Don't cry," my older half-brother, Doug, would counsel me. "It won't do any good."

He was right. I eventually tried to cope by having zero expectations about life. I shut down so that I wouldn't feel the pain that inevitably comes when you love someone.

But as a young boy, it was hard not to hope. Despite my certainty that my life would never be happy or stable like other people's, I always dreamed that things would be different. By the time I was a teenager, however, Simon and Garfunkel had arrived on the scene to capture my feelings in their famous song. I was a rock. I was an island.

I listened to Simon and Garfunkel over and over on my record turntable, watching the needle trace the grooves of the smooth black vinyl. *It's true*, I thought. *If you don't open yourself up to care for other people, you won't be disappointed.*

I believed that love was overrated anyway. My mother had chased after it all my life, and her search had taken me from place to place with no real rhyme or reason. I was looking for it, too: I tried to catch my mom's attention by being funny, and it felt good when I could make her laugh. But I never heard the words "I love you," and I sure didn't know how to express them to anyone else. I was an island.

Then I became a Christian. A new world opened up. No more island; I was on a vast new continent where love was real. I found it, felt it, saw it in my new friends at church. Then came Cathe . . . and I began to venture out more and more into the scary new world of loving, really loving, another person.

Cathe was—and is—beautiful, like my mother. But the similarities end there. Personality-wise, my mom ran hot or cold; Cathe runs consistent. My mom was given to fits of temper. Cathe is stable. Where my mom had no interest in spiritual things for most of her life, Cathe is a godly woman. She is a partner who counsels me, encourages me and puts me in my place when necessary.

From early on, she was not only my wife but also my best friend, and as our relationship grew, I was overwhelmed by the gift of Cathe by my side.

Then I became a father. Love became even more wonderful and terrifying as I looked down on the innocent faces of my baby sons in my arms.

With my wife and family, and in my church family, God gave me blessings I could not comprehend. I, who had felt like an outcast and an orphan for years, had loved ones, a home and a community of my own. I had come such a long, long way. God had been so good to me.

So I was surprised by how much my disappointment about Barney rocked me.

Here I was, entering the fifth decade of my life. But the fact that I meant nothing to my birth father, and that meeting him had meant very little to me, brought back waves of disappointment and pain I hadn't felt for years. I knew I had to take stock.

I fully realized that people would let me down. I knew that I failed others. Other people are flawed, and I'm flawed big-time. But in this situation with Barney, was I really feeling, down deep, that *God* had let me down?

When you're illegitimate, sometimes you wonder if you were ever even meant to be at all. I knew I was an "accident." Charlene did not earnestly hope and plan to conceive me. For all I know, she was drunk and had no memory of my conception. I'm immensely grateful that once she discovered she was pregnant, she did not choose to abort me.

But divinely speaking, I was no accident. God was present at my beginnings. He knew me before I was born. He knew then and knows now the number of the days I'll walk this earth. He provided for me—a messed-up mortal with questionable beginnings—so that I'll actually live forever with Him.

The psalmist wrote, "You watched me as I was being formed in utter seclusion, as I was woven together in the dark of the womb. You saw me before I was born. Every day of my life was recorded in your book. Every moment was laid out before a single day had passed. How precious are your thoughts about me, O God! They are innumerable!" (Ps. 139:15-17).

I would not wish my childhood on anyone. But it's the life I was given . . . and the very things that were the hardest were given to me so that I could understand the people I'm called to help.

The Bible tells the well-known story of Joseph, who came from a very dysfunctional home (see Gen. 37–50). His father, Jacob, doted on him; while Joseph's 11 brothers wore common, sleeveless tunics for manual labor, Jacob presented Joseph with a long-sleeved coat with many colors woven into it. It was the garment of the upper class. The other brothers, in their sweaty work uniforms, got the message. To make matters worse, Jacob sent Joseph to check up on his brothers, to see how their work was progressing. Then he'd report back to Dad.

One day Joseph's brothers had had enough. They ganged up on him and threw him into a pit. At first they were just going to teach him a lesson, but then a party of slave traders "just happened" by. The brothers made some cash and got rid of Joseph, all at once. A good day's work.

Sold into slavery in Egypt, Joseph grew from being a naïve young boy into a godly man. He suffered false charges of rape and a long imprisonment. But he grew in character and eventually took the notice of the most powerful man in the then-known world, the pharaoh. Joseph became prime minister of Egypt, second in command. Under his leadership, Egypt flourished.

In Act III of this tale, there was a famine in their land, so Joseph's brothers traveled from Canaan to Egypt to buy food. They were older and wiser, but they did not recognize their long-lost brother, now holding enormous power and wearing a King Tut outfit.

But Joseph recognized them. His heart ached. He didn't want revenge. Standing face to face with his past, he wanted a fresh future. After revealing his true identity to his flabbergasted brothers, Joseph broke into tears. He forgave them for trying to kill him. "You meant evil against me," he said. "But God meant it for good. . . . God did it!"

Joseph had been betrayed, slandered, falsely accused and incarcerated before things went well for him in Egypt. But he believed that God was at work in the bad as well as the good. He wasn't bitter.

Why had God allowed it? The Bible gives us the luxury of an answer: "to save many people alive" (Gen. 50:20, NKJV).

I'm no Joseph, but I can look back at my life and finally say the same thing. I wasn't a mistake. God had a purpose. My weird, dysfunctional upbringing prepared me—in ways that a happy childhood could not have—to bring the gospel to wounded people who come from chaotic backgrounds like my own . . . so that many could be saved.

I come back to the familiar words of Romans 8:28: "We know that God causes everything to work together for the good of those who love God and are called according to his purpose for them."

In the psalms, King David wrote to God, "Everything serves your plans!" (Ps. 119:91). He didn't mean that all things are pleasant. Life's experiences had been otherwise for him. But David knew that God is the King of the universe and uses everything for His mysterious purposes. Everything.

When I was a small boy, my grandmother would make biscuits for every meal. It was a Southern thing. I would watch Mama Stella hungrily; I knew how wonderful those biscuits tasted, steaming from the oven, dripping with sweet butter.

Mama Stella would get out a jug of cold buttermilk, a flask of vegetable oil and some self-rising flour. That was it. She never measured anything, but knew intuitively the right amounts of each ingredient. She mixed the dough gently until the ingredients just began to come together. Then she pinched off an individual portion, formed it into a circle, and tossed it lightly from hand to hand before she slipped it onto a blackened pan.

Then she popped the biscuits into a very, very hot oven.

I could not have stomached any of those ingredients on their own. Buttermilk? Forget it. Even after it was mixed with oil and flour, I couldn't have eaten the raw dough. But once those biscuits emerged from Mama Stella's oven, they were transformed, the stuff of legend.

The "everything" of Romans 8:28 is like the ingredients of biscuit dough. Trials and troubles are distasteful. We avoid them if possible. And we certainly recoil from the heat of the oven.

But God, in His infinite skill, blends all things in our lives and cooks them in the oven of adversity. One day we shall be able to see them fully transformed. Then we can *taste* that they are good. For now, we must believe it.

3 3

REPULLULAT: IT BUDS AFRESH

As you know, after Oscar Laurie adopted me and gave me his name, I began to feel a new sense of stability. A new name. A new home. I could put down my roots.

Then my mom left him and swept me off to Hawaii. I felt chopped off. I was like a dry stump.

But God was doing something.

I thought of those days during the horrific California wildfires last year. Areas of our state looked like the end of the world. Ash rained down on our doorsteps and the skies were black with smoke from canyons full of fire. Whipped by the wind, the flames spiraled out of control to engulf homes, parks and acres of forests; afterward, there were only cinders, rising smoke and falling ash.

Later, police identified several arsonists who admitted to setting small fires. One was a boy who had no idea that his spark would blaze into a killer inferno. Wildfires like that can also begin naturally. When the forests are dry in the summers, the Santa Ana winds blow hot and fierce; any lightning strike can end in conflagration.

Many plant species actually depend on fire as a means to reproduce. Some pine trees produce cones whose seeds are locked in by a resinous coating that is melted away in a fire. The seeds need heat to be released.

Other plants, such as Coast Live Oaks, are able to do what scientists call "stump sprouting." When the branches and trunks of these trees burn, only stumps are left. But the heat of the fire stimulates the deep, unseen, undamaged taproot that nourishes the tree. It causes the stump to send out new growth . . . little, tender green sprouts that emerge from the gnarled, dead-looking stub.

When I reconnected with Oscar Laurie as an adult, he told me one day how the Laurie family name originated in Scotland around the time of the Norman Conquest. He showed me our family crest, and I discovered that the Lauries count the legendary Scotsman William Wallace, of *Braveheart* fame, as an ancestor. I had never known such heraldry existed.

The crest is red, black and gold with a knight's silver visor and a goblet that holds a crown made of laurel leaves. At the top there's a brown tree stump. It's been hacked off, and there are tiny stems of new green growth shooting out of the near-dead wood.

Stump sprouting, nourished by the taproot.

"That goes with the Laurie family motto," said Oscar. "It's Latin. *Repullulat*. It means 'It buds afresh.'"

I looked at the lined, kind face of the man who adopted me, and thought about new life springing out of what looked absolutely dead.

"I get it," I said, putting my arm around his shoulder. "Kind of like my life, right?"

He smiled and nodded. "Yes, son. Mine, too."

The end.

LOST AND FOUND

I told you at the beginning of this book that I would try not to preach. That's hard for a guy who's a pastor/evangelist! But at this point I'd be remiss if I didn't talk to you directly a little bit and let you know how my story just might connect with yours in a way that can bring new hope to your life if you need it.

It's a story that Jesus told about another lost boy.

Unlike me, this boy had a hands-on, loving father. (Nothing is said of a mother.)

Though his father was kind, nurturing and gave the boy rules to live by, this crazy kid could not get out of the house fast enough. He is better known as "the prodigal son," and for centuries people have told his story.

But it's actually not so much about the son. Jesus told this story so that we could get a picture of what *God* is like.

Here's how Jesus told the tale:

A man had two sons.

The younger son told his father, "I want my share of your estate now, instead of waiting until you die." So his father agreed to divide his wealth between his sons.

A few days later this younger son packed all his belongings and took a trip to a distant land, and there he wasted all his money on wild living.

About the time his money ran out, a great famine swept over the land, and he began to starve. He persuaded a local farmer to hire him to feed his pigs. The boy became so hungry that even the pods he was feeding the pigs looked good to him. But no one gave him anything.

When he finally came to his senses, he said to himself, "At home even the hired men have food enough to spare, and here I am, dying of hunger! I will go home to my father and say, 'Father, I have sinned against both heaven and you, and I am no longer worthy of being called your son. Please take me on as a hired man.'".

So he returned home to his father. And while he was still a long distance away, his father saw him coming. Filled with love and compassion, he ran to his son, embraced him, and kissed him.

His son said to him, "Father, I have sinned against both heaven and you, and I am no longer worthy of being called your son."

But his father said to the servants, "Quick! Bring the finest robe in the house and put it on him. Get a ring for his finger, and sandals for his feet. And kill the calf we have been fattening in the pen. We must celebrate with a feast, for this son of mine was dead and has now returned to life. He was lost, but now he is found."

So the party began (Luke 15:12-24).

You know, sin is such a rip-off. It promises good times, and the Bible acknowledges that there is "pleasure in sin for a time" (Heb. 11:25). But eventually, sin brings misery.

I had some fun times before I was a believer. But I had far, far more times of misery, emptiness and a dead feeling of meaninglessness.

The prodigal son in Jesus' story left home with a spring in his step and money in his pockets. When he got to Hollywood, or New York, or whatever the big town was in his day, he had a lot of new friends.

But as soon as his money ran out, his friends ran out with it.

This kid sank so low that he took the only job he could find: working for a farmer feeding his pigs. This was not an appropriate job for a good Jewish boy.

Then one day, he came to his senses and realized that he had it better in his father's house than he did in this pigsty. (Genius.) It was time to go home.

In my case, there were little glimpses of the good life, back when I was young. When I'd go to church with my grandparents, I'd see God for a second, or when I heard Billy Graham preach on their old TV. When I was a teenager, movies that had Jesus in them, such as *Ben Hur*, moved me for no apparent reason.

And then on my high school campus, I came to my senses, like the prodigal.

I entertained thoughts that were new to me. *What if these Christians are actually right and it is I who is wrong?* I thought. That was new. And then when the preacher guy said that Jesus said people were either for Him or against Him, that hit me.

I did not want be against Jesus. When I was honest, I felt that Jesus had been for me all my life. He had protected me when I could have died any number of times.

That prodigal son said to himself, "I will go home to my father and say, 'Father, I have sinned against both heaven and you, and I am no longer worthy of being called your son. Please take me on as a hired man.'"

Now, he could have sat there in the pigpen and said that to himself for weeks.

Months.

Years.

It's not enough to know you need to get right with God. You need to act on it.

So, the boy got up, and he headed home.

Though the son had sinned and dragged the family name through the gutter, the father still loved him. Now getting on in years, he'd sit out on his front porch and hope and wait. He wanted his son back home, with him, but in order for it to be a happy return, the son needed to change.

One day, as the father sat down in his worn chair and looked down the long path leading to his home. He saw the thin silhouette of what looked like a man.

The father leaned forward and squinted to make out the form. It was unmistakable.

It was his son!

The father leapt from his chair with joy. He jumped down the porch steps and ran toward his son.

What was going through the prodigal's mind at this point? *The old man is so mad, he can't wait to get his hands around my throat!*

No. The boy knew better.

His father reached him and threw his arms around him and kissed him over and over, in spite of the fact that the kid was dirty and smelled like ripe pigs.

Then the boy began his well-rehearsed speech: "Father, I have sinned against both heaven and you, and I am no longer worthy of being called your son . . ."

The father hugged him tight and called the servants. "Quick! Bring the finest robe in the house and put it on him. Get a ring for his finger, and sandals for his feet."

This meant the prodigal was being returned to full sonship, with all its legal rights.

All was forgiven.

The father exuberantly called for the feast. "We must celebrate!" he shouted. "This son of mine was dead and now he's alive!"

The lost boy was found.

Down deep, no matter how sophisticated or tough we may appear on the outside, we're all lost boys and girls. We're all searching for meaning and purpose in life. We all want to be found.

Your Father, who loves you more than you can dream, is waiting for you to come home.

But how do you do that?

First, you must admit that you are a sinner.

In Jesus' story, the father accepted the son as he was, but he didn't leave him that way. God is waiting for you to come home to Him. You don't have to try to clean your life up first. Just come . . . and then God will help you clean up your life.

But you must first admit that you are a sinner.

A lot of people choke on that word. When we think "sinner," we think of criminals. Murderers. Abusers. Yes, they are sinners. But you are, too. The Bible says that "Everyone has sinned; we all fall short of God's glorious standard" (Rom. 3:23).

The word "sin" has many meanings in the Bible. One meaning is to "cross the line." We have all done that. If you read the Ten Commandments, all of us have broken at least one of them. If not far more.

You might protest and say, "Well, I'm not as bad as some people!" And that may be true. But God does not grade on the curve. One sin is enough to keep you out of heaven. The Bible says, "The person who keeps all of the laws except one is as guilty as a person who has broken all of God's laws" (Jas. 2:10).

Another way the Bible uses the word "sin" means to "miss the mark." God has set a standard for all of humanity. It's called *perfection*. Jesus said, "You are to be perfect, even as your Father in heaven is perfect" (Matt. 5:48).

Now, who can measure up to that? I can't.

Nor can you. That's where Jesus comes in.

Second, you must realize that Jesus Christ died on the cross for you.

Jesus was more then a good man. He was the God man. Not a man becoming God—that's impossible—but God becoming a man. That is why Jesus, and He alone, was uniquely qualified to bridge the gap between a holy, perfect God and human beings who fall short of His perfection.

Jesus, being fully God and fully man, died for our sins. The Bible says, "God showed his great love for us by sending Christ to die for us while we were still sinners" (Rom. 5:8).

With one hand Jesus took hold of that holy God, and with the other hand He took hold of sinful humanity, and cruel spikes were driven in as He died in our place on a Roman cross. He gave Himself as a sacrifice for your sins and mine, because there was no other way to satisfy God's righteous requirements.

Jesus lived a life of perfect righteousness, a life we could not live, and He paid a debt He did not owe, because we owed a debt we could not pay.

What do you do about this?

Third, you must repent of your sin.

Admitting you are a sinner is the beginning; now you need to repent.

That's such an old-fashioned word . . . what does it really mean? It means to be sorry, sorry enough to stop doing what grieves God the Father's heart. The Bible says that "the kind of sorrow God wants us to experience leads us away from sin and results in salvation. There's no regret for that kind of sorrow" (2 Cor. 7:10). It also tell us that God "commands everyone everywhere to repent of their sins and turn to him" (Acts 17:30).

We must change our direction. It's like hanging a U-turn on the road of life. It's like the prodigal getting up, changing direction from his former ways, and heading home. It's like me: When I first heard all this as a 17-year-old, I knew it was time to turn from this old lifestyle I had been living.

You must be willing to turn from all known sin.

And fourth, you must receive Jesus Christ as Savior and Lord.

Jesus, who died on the cross and received the punishment for your sin and mine, rose from the dead three days later.

Incredible.

Now He waits at the entrance of your life. Here's what He says: "I stand at the door and knock. If anyone hears My voice and opens the door, I will come in to him and dine with him, and he with Me" (Rev. 3:20, *NKJV*). Will you open the door of your heart to Him? It's a decision only you can make. No one else can make it for you.

In my case, my grandmother took me to church as a boy, but she could not make me a believer. I had to make that choice myself, and you need to do the same.

Jesus is a gentleman. He will not force His way into your life. But I must warn you: Not saying yes to Him is, by default, saying no. Not to decide is to decide. Jesus said, "Anyone who isn't with me opposes me, and anyone who isn't working with me is actually working against me" (Matt. 12:30). To work against Him means that you will face all eternity separated from God in a very real place called hell.

The last thing God wants is for any man or woman uniquely created in His own image to spend eternity separated from Him in hell. That is why Jesus paid such a drastic price on the cross: so that we can go to heaven.

Are you trying to fill a void in your life with the things this world has to offer? Friend, you were created to know God. And you can come into a relationship with Him right now, just like I did, and countless others. God is only a prayer away.

If you want Christ to come into your life right now to forgive you of your sin . . . if you want your guilt removed and to have a fresh start in life . . . if you want to go to heaven when you die . . . you can pray a simple, sincere prayer, and God will change your life.

Lord Jesus, I know that I am a sinner. I am sorry.
I thank You for dying on the cross for my sins, and I turn from that sin now
and ask You to come into my life as Savior and Lord.
I choose to follow You from this day forward all the days of my life.
Thank You for calling me and accepting me.
In Jesus' name I pray. Amen.

Again, that's a really simple prayer. But it's a new beginning, and if you meant it, Jesus Christ has just come into your life. You may feel tearful or excited, or you may not feel anything at all. But the point of this is not how you feel, but what God has just done in you. He says in the Bible that you have become a new person!

WE MUST BE WILLING TO BEAR THE CROSS TO WEAR THE CROWN

TRIALS / ETERNAL LIFE

GOD IS WILLING THAT ALL SHOULD COME TO REPENTENCE, GOD DOES'NT SEND ANYONE TO HELL - WE DECIDE OUR ETERNAL DESTINY! JESUS DIED SO WE COULD BE SET FREE FROM THE BONDAGE OF SIN!

WHY DON'T YOU GET LIBERATED FROM SIN AND TAKE A DRINK OF LIVING WATER? SPIRITUAL REFRESHMENT COMES FROM THE LORD! ASK JESUS IN YOUR HEART AND FIND ETERNAL PEACE WITH GOD!

THINK ABOUT WHAT JESUS SAID, BEFORE YOU LET YOUR MIND REJECT HIM - LISTEN TO YOUR HEART INSTEAD AND YOU WILL ACCEPT HIM!

NOW IF YOU'VE RECEIVED JESUS

TIPS FOR GROWTH ... #1 READ THE BIBLE

#2 PRAY & PRAISE "PRAY WITHOUT CEASING" 1 THES 5.17 "LET EVERYTHING THAT HAS BREATH PRAISE YE THE LORD PSALMS 150.6

#3 WITNESS "DO THE WORK OF AN EVANGELIST"

#4 FELLOWSHIP "FORSAKE NOT THE ASSEMBLING OF THE SAINTS" JESUS

APPENDIX

LOST BOYS AND LOST GIRLS:
THEIR STORIES

Perhaps you are thinking, *That is nice what God did for Greg, but I'm not an artist or a preacher and the Jesus Movement is long past.* You have read my story. But it does not end with the last chapter. When God gets involved, the story goes on and it becomes other people's stories, too. The important part isn't a lost boy named Greg who God found and turned around. It's about all of us and what we can become.

Almost every day I get moving letters or phone calls about big turnarounds in people's lives. So rather than me going on about my story—which does go on!—I want to share the stories of some other lost boys and lost girls who have been found. All of the following have been adapted from real letters that I have received from real people, some of whom have stories just like yours. They were lost, but now they are found.

* * *

Hi Pastor Greg,

Ten years ago, Sandy (now my wife) and I were both drug addicts and alcoholics. We had been on a party binge for five days with no sleep. On our fifth day of no sleep, we were high on drugs and we wanted to get out of the house.

Back then, the rock and roll station was located right next to the Christian station. I recalled hearing a little something on the radio concerning something called a Harvest Crusade. We thought it was a farmer's convention with country music and that sort of thing. The Harvest bumper stickers were on cars all over the place, and that year they had wheat on them, so we were certain we were headed to a hoe-down with all the fixins! We had no money and figured we could stomach a little country (in lieu of our traditional heavy metal) for some free food. Little did we know how well we were going to be fed.

We called the stadium where the crusade was being held and they confirmed that it was free, so off we went. We were two of the first people standing at the gate. In our own little world, we were oblivious to people carrying Bibles. We didn't talk to anyone and we still had no idea that this event had anything to do with God. We were clueless.

Once the gates opened, we found seats in the very front row. I remember looking around at all of the smiling people and really tripping. It didn't seem real, but it was rather cool.

Brad and I both were doing drugs in the bathroom inside of the stadium. When the music started I turned around and saw a bunch of happy, clapping people. I wanted to be happy, too.

When you started your message, we felt you were literally looking right at us. When you gave the invitation to ask Jesus into our hearts, we both got up at the same time, looked at each other without saying a word and walked out on the field. After praying, we immediately sobered up. We even went back to the crusade the next night.

That was 10 years ago. We have been walking with the Lord ever since. And we go to Harvest Crusades whenever we can. In fact, we have had Harvest Crusade parties when we've invited all of our old party friends, drug dealers included. We have food and games and then caravan to the stadium. We partied for over 13 years with a big group of friends and now more than half of us have come to the Lord. Two of our former drug dealers are now walking with Jesus.

—Brad and Sandy

*   *   *

Dear Greg Laurie,

Years ago, I said a sinner's prayer in my room in college at the prompting of my Christian girlfriend. I thought I was set, but in retrospect, my life certainly didn't reflect a commitment to Christ. I read the Bible by day and got drunk with my fraternity brothers at night. I know . . . not a very good witness at all. I was still a very lost boy.

After graduating college, I heard the Harvest Crusades were coming to Rochester, where I lived. I thought it would be great to go, so I brought my girlfriend. I heard an amazing message about repentance and sin and judgment.

That night, my life came crashing down on me. What if I wasn't actually a Christian? What if for the past year and a half I'd been putting on a good show, but there was no change in my heart and I didn't have the Holy Spirit in me? You gave the invitation to make a commitment to follow Jesus Christ, and I stood up and asked my girlfriend (now my wife) to come with me. I remember exactly where I was sitting. I remember walking down the steps and going through each landing and walking onto the floor of the arena. I remember thinking that nothing mattered at all in the world except getting right with God—that sinful self I was struggling with was no longer going to control me. While normally I'd be embarrassed, I remember thinking, *I don't care what people think.*

Before that night, it never occurred to me that I should find a church. After the crusade, I started to go to two weekly Bible studies. I grew quickly and earnestly with the Lord.

A couple years later, I became active in a prison ministry and have been going nearly weekly since then to preach the gospel to prisoners. I've been so privileged to pray the sinner's prayer with hundreds of them. I hope you don't mind, but I often use your words to describe myself: *I'm just one beggar telling another beggar where to find food.*

—Christopher

*   *   *

Dear Greg,

In July 1995, one of my sisters, her husband and my mother invited me to go to the Harvest Crusade. At that time I had no idea what it was—maybe just a bunch of Christians getting together and singing. I figured I would humor them as long as they did not expect me to sing. I had always believed in Jesus as my Savior, but I was leaving the commitment part until I was old and my life was closer to the end.

I felt a little out of place, but the music was great. It was the first time I heard Crystal Lewis and the band Love Song. I had a difficult time listening to some of the messages given that night because of the life I was living at the time. But you were the one who God used to speak to me.

I will forever remember your words that night. You asked the question, "If God came tonight, would you be ready to go?" I knew what the answer was, but I could not admit it to myself. At that moment, I made eye contact with my mother and I was caught off guard. I looked at her and tears built up in her eyes. I could hear "Welcome Back" by Love Song playing in the background. She finally asked if I wanted to go down to the field, and I said yes.

It was so emotional—my mom and sister were in tears, and we all began walking to the field. We were up in the very top level, in the nosebleed section, so the walk to the field seemed to take forever. All I could hear was the song and the words "Welcome back to where you once belonged." I know it was Jesus speaking those words to me. During my walk, I thought back over my life and the choices I had made and the trials I had faced and the times I felt so alone . . .

Needless to say, I grew up feeling like an outcast. Most of my childhood, from what I remember, I felt unaccepted, and I put my attention toward academics and did very well until I went to high school.

By then, it was so important to me that I fit in with a crowd. I decided I would do whatever it took to fit in. Of course, I discovered partying. It began with having a drink. From the age of 14 to 23, it evolved into experimenting with drugs and sex. Before long, I was able to justify the attractions I had by calling myself "bisexual."

After high school, I went into the military. While in basic training, I went to Sunday services. It was the only time during those six weeks that I felt at peace. I look back and realize that God was calling me back, but I was too blind to see it. During my four years in the military, I convinced myself that my past was all about experimenting and I was now over it.

Three years later, I got married to a girl I knew in high school. I knew that I was not ready to be married, but I felt it would keep me from being pulled back into my past lifestyle. Needless to say, it did not last more than six months.

Soon I was single again and out of the military, and ready to do as I pleased. It was not long until I was hanging out with people who enjoyed partying. At 24, I gave into my temptations and fell for the lie that homosexuality is the way some people are born. I also started to believe that God would not hold it against me, so I stepped into a life that accepted this lifestyle.

I thought I was having a great time. I met people in the entertainment industry, hung out with doctors, and went to some very nice places. Now I can see how the enemy used those things to make me believe I was happy.

This brings me to July 1995, walking to the field of Edison Stadium at the age of 31, with my mom on one side and one of my sisters on the other. They were both in tears and I could only think, *I know my life is going to change; do I want it to?*

Eight years later, I have never regretted my decision that night. If we take the step to follow Christ, He will make changes in our lives. Today, I am celebrating my seven-year anniversary with my beautiful wife, a strong Christian woman. We have begun a ministry at our church. We have two beautiful children: a son who is six who has a great love for our Lord Jesus and a two-year-old daughter who already says a prayer for dinner and who knows that church is about God.

God has put these people in my life to help me stay focused and to remember to thank Him for all His blessings. Obstacles still come along my path and I realize I will have trials until I leave this earth. But I also know when I do leave and I open my eyes, Jesus will be standing there waiting to answer my questions and to tell me, "Welcome back."

May God continue to always bless you.

—David

*   *   *

Dear Greg,

This year has been the most amazing spiritual time of my family's life. It began with my son questioning if God exists, saw me start nursing school, and climaxed with us attending the Harvest Crusade in Anaheim.

At about this time, my son battled with suicidal feelings. He had a 4.3 GPA and nothing to be depressed about, yet he wanted to end his life. I kept telling him to have faith in the Lord and everything would fall into place. He was reluctant to believe.

A Christian girl at my son's school also talked to him about God. When my son told me, I was excited that God had a plan. Then a friend invited me to your crusade in Anaheim. I took my whole family. The kids were reluctant to go and I almost folded, but I knew that God had something in store for us. So we went to the crusade. My children sat there as if they were going to have their teeth pulled. When the music began, I turned to look at my kids and saw that they were still all sitting like three bumps on a log!

I refused to worry and instead waited. The next time I looked, all of the kids were standing, singing the songs and praising God. This was the most incredible day that our family has ever had.

In the middle of the service, my son said, "Mom, what does it mean up on the screen? It says today you can change your life." I explained that many people would go down to the field and give their lives to the Lord. Guess what? Because of what Greg Laurie said, because of the music played, because we believed in our Lord to act, our entire family became Christians that day!

—DeeDee

* * *

Dear Greg,

I grew up in Southern California after moving here from Cleveland, Ohio, in 1975 with my family; I was five years old and the youngest of three boys. Our family lived in a nice house, drove great cars and fawned over a sheep dog named Patches.

For my dad, alcohol with friends turned to marijuana, marijuana turned to cocaine, cocaine turned to freebasing, freebasing turned into heroin, heroin turned into selling drugs, selling drugs turned into living on the streets, living on the streets turned him into a bum getting food out of trash cans, and that brought him home seeking self-help. And every time he tried to do it on his own, Dad went back to drugs. Eventually his seven counts of drunk driving caught up with him and put him in jail for three years.

I hated my father with all of my heart and wanted to kill him for hurting my mom and brothers. I watched my mom work full-time to take care of our basic needs and try so hard to keep it all together while hiding our pain from the world.

During this long cycle of self-destruction with my father, sin was beginning to be passed on to me. I had the "privilege" of doing cocaine with my father, going on a drug run with my father, lying and covering for my father, hitting my father so he would not drive drunk, catching my father doing drugs, and having strangers with guns in the house. I saw my dad beaten from head to toe, lying on blood-soaked sheets, my money stolen—my money needed for rent and food. (Football coaches gave me money from Coke machines at school to buy food because I couldn't count on or trust my father.)

Dad missed my eleventh, twelfth and thirteenth birthdays, as well as my graduation from Marine Corps boot camp.

My insecure and uncertain childhood caused me to have a very independent attitude: I was going to make it through life on my own. I focused all my attention on girls, football, beer and parties.

But God put a girl in my life named Kimberly. Kim grew up in the church but had fallen away. Her parents were still involved, and one Sunday night invited us to a church in Huntington Beach. I liked the band and the music, but I thought I was too cool to worship at the time. After the service, I asked the pastor a lot of why-this and why-that questions and he took the time to answer them.

It was August, and I was in the Marine Corp, slotted to go to Iraq during Desert Storm. My older brother, Robert, had recently become a Christian and dragged me to the Harvest Crusade at the Pacific Amphitheater. I went every night, and on the last night I made the greatest decision of my life. On August 18, I found out the meaning of life: having a relationship with God. I went forward and made a commitment to follow Jesus Christ.

That was 14 years ago, and today I proclaim a miracle. God gave me grace for all that I had done wrong, and once I started on the path of trying to lead a God-centered life, I have received one continuous blessing after another and been given the desires of my heart.

Kimberly and I are now married and have five beautiful children. I am in full-time ministry. My dad accepted Christ at El Cajon jail in San Diego and God delivered him from all of his addictions. Dad started volunteering at ALANO clubs and speaking at men's breakfasts, conferences and retreats. He now heads the restoration ministry at a local church. Mom moved back from Ohio after four years. Dad rebuilt his relationship with his boys and wife and now we all live in South Orange County and see each other on a regular basis.

Thirteen years ago, my family was broken and the epitome of dysfunction, but as we read in Psalm 40:1, "I waited patiently for the LORD; he turned to me and heard my cry."

—Gregg

* * *

Hi Greg,

My name's Jackie. I'm 20 years old and recently welcomed God into my life. Like most people in college, I was all about the parties, drinking, living a crazy lifestyle and not really focusing on my future. I kept my last job secret from most of my family because I was working in an adult bookstore, a disgrace to the family. It was a huge burden on me to lie about my place of work and I wanted to change but I needed another job before quitting.

My mom told me about the Harvest Crusade coming up. She said it would be fun because there would be bands, skateboarders, and it would be something new to try. I wasn't so sure about that, but I was looking for something different, so I agreed to go.

To my surprise, I loved it. The moment that really opened my heart was when you called for all those in the crowd that would like to start over and have God in their lives to walk onto the field. I was on the very top level with my mom, her boyfriend and my little cousin, waiting to see if they were going to walk down. I waited a few minutes and it was obvious they weren't going, so I decided to stay put, too. After a few more moments, I had this overwhelming sense that I wanted to join the people on the field, but I thought it was already too late. I tried to hold back a bit longer, but the pull felt so strong inside me that I knew that if I didn't go I'd regret it.

see you making your way down, we'll wait for you." At that moment, I
stood up and asked my little cousin to come with me. She agreed and
then we walked down. After the crusade, I immediately quit my job,
moved into a new house with an aunt and uncle who have a strong commitment to Christ, and started taking classes in real estate. I recently
passed the state exam. I know none of this would have been possible if
I had stayed up there in the bleachers.

—Jackie

* * *

Dear Pastor Greg,

Our second child was just born, and we had a lot of questions about
life. A relative who had been a heroin addict and an alcoholic had come
to the Lord, and, for lack of a better description, you could see Jesus all
over her. Everything about her changed, and she had a different attitude toward others than she used to have.

That relative invited us to attend a Harvest Crusade in Visalia, in
central California, in 1998. To be truthful, we only went as a gesture of
encouragement for her. Neither of us knew that the other had been
searching, wondering and asking questions. And neither of us knew
that as the Crusade began, God would tug at both of our hearts.

Sorry to say, we don't remember your message, but we do remember God's presence and going forward in unison—no words were shared
as we both rose and walked to the field.

That was 1998, and since that time we have grown as followers of
Christ. We are now in the ministry. No one has to go through life lost,
with unanswered questions. Jesus promises that if we will ask Him into
our lives and follow Him, He has made a place for each of us.

—Gary and Sophia

*   *   *

Dear Pastor Greg,

Eleven years ago, at a Harvest Crusade in Anaheim Stadium, you delivered a message on the subject of death. In attendance was my family, including my 11-year-old son, Timothy. It was a compelling message, and when you gave an invitation to accept Jesus Christ, my son asked, "Dad, are we going to go forward?"

I prayed (very quickly), and then I told him, "Each of us must make his own decision to follow Christ and I made that decision a number of years ago. It's your decision and I will support you." I bowed my head again and prayed, this time for my son. He stood up and held out his hand and asked me to go with him to the field. With tears in my eyes, I walked to the grassy outfield of Anaheim Stadium, where my son dedicated his life to Jesus Christ as his Lord and Savior.

On August 3, 2004, Timothy suddenly died in an accident. He was only 22 years old. I wanted you to know that you and the Harvest Crusade were used by God to bring the gospel message to my son. We have the assurance of being with him again in heaven, a gift beyond measure.

We are very much in debt to the Harvest family for the comfort they have provided to our family during this crisis. Truly, what the world meant for harm, God meant for good. We have many praise reports during the past several weeks, not the least being that my 11-year-old son, Lucas, has made a commitment to Jesus Christ as his Lord and Savior. Praise God!

—Ray

*   *   *

Dear Greg Laurie,

I am happily married to a wonderful Christian man. I have two sweet little ones, and I wanted to thank you for your ministry. Fifteen years ago at the Aloha Stadium, I dedicated my life to Christ. I was 19, living on my own, thinking I knew it all. Looking back on it, I was in my own personal hell.

One day, a guy came up to me and told me he knew of a great concert at the Aloha Stadium. He asked me along. I jumped at the chance for a free concert, little knowing what was about to happen. We weren't there but a little while when I began to feel the presence of the Holy Spirit in that place. I still remember looking up into the sky and never in my life feeling so close to God.

I grew up in a very ritualistic mainline denominational home and had never even heard the message about having a "personal relationship" with God. Needless to say, when Greg gave the invitation, I felt led to get up and go down to the field.

Obviously, my life has never been the same. A few weeks ago, my five-year-old son and I watched this years' Harvest Crusade, and at the end I just started bawling. My son asked me why I was crying, and I shared with him that I was saved at one of these events. I am his Sunday School teacher, and he is very much aware of salvation. I can't wait for his day to come.

—Teresa

* * *

Dear Greg,

I had a terrible childhood that included alcohol, drugs, hard-rock music, self-mutilation, lots of psychotherapy and many failures in school. I graduated high school with a 2.0 average, thanks only to sports and playing drums. I wanted to be a SEAL team member in the U.S. Navy, but was turned down and became a rescue swimmer instead.

While in the military, I continued to drink heavily and even use drugs that my buddies and I smuggled across the border. It was the way of life in the military, both overseas and in the States. I got married only two weeks after I met the woman who is now my wife. I didn't know if

I liked her or hated her. We even lived in separate cities. When I got out of the military, I was proud and arrogant, had an addiction to alcohol and wanted an annulment. We fought all the time. I tried to force my wife to have an abortion, literally twisting her arm and pushing her face against the coffee table. In that moment, I could have been even more violent; instead, I put my fist through a wall.

Not long after that, understandably my wife packed her bags to go home to New York. My mom invited us to dinner and said we would go to a short concert before eating. I hated the music and tried to ignore your teachings, but some things did make sense. With your last call to come down for the invitation of salvation, I said to God, *If You are real, my wife will go first.* She grew up a non-practicing Catholic and didn't care if there was a God—I was pretty sure I was safe.

But then she grabbed my hand and led me down to the field. I clung to my wife with hurt, shame, guilt, appreciation and the comfort of accepting Jesus as my Savior.

We just celebrated our eighth year of marriage and continue to serve God with music, youth ministry, children's ministry and missions trips to Mexico, Nicaragua and the streets of Southern California. And now God has called me to be a pastor/teacher with a desire to have a church plant!

May the grace of Jesus be with you and your family.

—Richard

* * *

Dear Greg,

My two daughters and I had just gone through a very difficult time with a daycare situation. In this process, I had a nervous breakdown and lost everything—literally. We moved in with my grandmother and tried to put the pieces of our lives back together. It was a struggle just for me to get up in the morning, let alone take a shower, eat or even brush my teeth. I had just fallen apart and my vices (smoking cigarettes and pot) had taken over my life along with the grief of knowing that I had taken my two-year-old daughter to this daycare for two years and they had been abusing her. I was consumed with sorrow, despair, depression and just outright darkness. It felt like a vacuum had sucked up my soul and all that I was.

In a deep moment of torment, I was in the fetal position on the floor and cried out to God, telling Him that He could not exist if things like this could occur. Total darkness seemed to surround me, welcoming me in this misery. But at the same time, there was this little tug at my heart that said, *On the contrary, I am real . . . just seek Me and you will see.* I stayed in that darkness for a while, but that voice kept calling to me: *Seek Me and I will show you who I am.*

One day, sitting outside my grandmother's house (as I did every day, smoking cigarettes and pot, unshowered and distraught with my plight), I found a Bible a friend had given to me 10 years before, so I began to read it. This was the first time I saw some light in months and the more I read, the more I wanted to know.

At about the same time, my 13-year-old daughter, Jacklyn, went to a Harvest Crusade with a friend and made a decision to follow Christ. She came home excited and told me about her experience in great detail, but I just shrugged my shoulders and turned the other way.

Jacklyn started going to the church around the corner and every Sunday she asked me to go. At first I said no, but something was happening to me, and I kept reading the Bible. I even began to pray to God. It was like the peeling of an onion: One layer at a time, the Lord took the hardness of my heart (all the horrible things in my life that had happened) and showed me what these feelings were and why they were there. Then He would say, "You don't need this anymore; give it to Me." Slowly but surely, my heart began to become softer and less filled with the dirt that had been put in there.

Finally, I told my daughter I would love to go to church. That was tough to do, because in my mind committing to God required total surrender. I also really didn't want people asking me questions about my life.

Somehow I managed to muster up enough courage to walk across the street, through the doors and into the last pew. I sat quietly with my little daughter and as soon as the service was over, I ran out the back door and back home.

I kept reading the Bible, and God started taking away some of my bad habits. My heart began to heal and open wide enough to let Him in. For the first time in my life I became whole. As my heart began to heal, I realized that not only was there enough room for God, but now I had an abundance of love to share with everyone I knew and met. I was no longer afraid of the people at church or anywhere. The love of God radiated through me, and everyone saw that transformation.

—Carol

* * *

Dear Pastor Greg,

I had a crazy past. I grew up in the drug scene—I started doing drugs when I was eight and got hooked on them when I was twelve. I kept using them all the way up until my twenties, when I gave my life to the Lord at the 1994 Harvest Crusade.

My brother had invited me and a friend to that crusade. I came not because I really wanted to know Jesus, but because I wanted to see the pretty girl my brother had invited! But then it was pretty simple. I answered the call. I gave my life over to Christ.

My start as a Christian was kind of rocky. I was living at a drug house, had to go to jail, and ended up in a men's home. The Lord kind of worked with me there. I have been in ministry ever since. And the pretty girl I wanted to meet? She is now my wife of eleven years.

—Steve

*   *   *

Dear Pastor Greg,

I was backslidden and stuck in an abusive relationship. Not only that, but I had accepted that I was going to die by the hand of my husband. I didn't care anymore about anything. Getting high was my only source of escape. I no longer knew how to even think properly. I was drowning in an ocean of hate, being tossed by the enemy's chaos. My life was one huge void!

I attended the Harvest Crusade in July 1996. My abusive husband made me go with him (ironic, right?). I thought to myself, *This is going to be so boring, but I'll just go; it'll be over soon.* I was high that night at the crusade. I had no intention of giving up my only source of escape (drugs) or changing my lifestyle. I was pretty set on dying where I was at in life—and soon! I had tried to escape the hands of my abuser and failed time and time again. I had given up hope for a real life.

At the crusade that night, I found myself lifting up my hands in praise to God through the music (The Kry) that was playing. It was cool music, not boring like I had always experienced, and then you made me laugh and think. God kept my attention all night long. It was joy I have never known.

All of my family went to the field at the invitation that night, and we gave our lives to Christ. Someone gave me a little Bible. My immediate thought was, *What do you want me to do with this . . . you actually want me to read?* But at that moment, I purposed in my heart to read that small Bible, the New Testament.

As I began to read Matthew 1, I realized that this book was about Jesus! I had no idea that's what the Bible was about. I had no idea that Jesus had a family tree. I never knew He became man and walked this earth. I didn't have a clue! I had heard about Jesus, but I thought He was just God in heaven. What a revelation. I began to read and read and read and read. What a transformation my life took because of what I discovered in the pages of that wonderful Bible. Jesus truly became my personal Savior and Lord after I learned about His life, death and resurrection.

His strength in my life is so amazing. Just like for the Israelites, He held back the waves of the sea of distress for me and I walked safely on dry ground to the promised land. I had been an abused woman for six years. I turned to drugs for comfort and escape. I lost my individuality, personality and the love of my children in those years. I couldn't think properly or clearly. I hated all mankind and was bitter toward everything and everyone. My family turned their backs on me in my time of need. They did not want to deal with such a mess. My father said to me, "Everyone has to die sometime" and my mother told me, "I forgot to tell you, you are not welcome here anymore."

I was so hurt and forsaken by everyone I knew that I blamed the whole world for my horrible life. Yet I also felt that I was such a bad person and didn't deserve any kind of real love at all. I believed that even God hated me and that's why I never got any relief anywhere. But that's not what I read in the Bible. The Bible told me that God loved me, even me! I had found a joy through God's Word that I wasn't ready to stop feeling and I knew that drugs would take that away.

God told me to be strong and of good courage and do not fear (that was a difficult thing to do—not to fear), so I strengthened myself in the Lord. God told me He had a plan for my life. His plan was one of good and not of evil. (Boy, that was a radical statement for me to read and believe! But it gave me hope that I have never known.)

God delivered me out of Egypt, out of the house of bondage, and now I have no other God before Him! I've been dwelling in God's Word on a daily basis ever since then. He has become my God!

—Tammy

*   *   *

Dear Harvest Crusade,

I dedicated my life to Jesus Christ back in 1976 at Calvary Chapel. Then came my senior year of high school, a bad-influence boyfriend, and just general wandering away from church. I had fallen away.

In 1991, I read an article in the newspaper about the Harvest Crusade that year. I remembered my Saturday nights as a teen at Calvary Chapel fondly, but I filed the information in the back of my head with an "I'm too busy to go" attitude.

Then came the night of the Crusade. It was about two minutes before the start, and I was close by. I drove into the parking lot thinking I would never find a space. Yet I pulled in easily. I walked into the amphitheater, thinking that it would be too crowded and I would never find a seat. But I got one in the orchestra pit.

My old pastor from Calvary Chapel Downey was speaking. Then came Pastor Chuck, speaking like a dear old dad, and I just started to weep. Then Greg spoke about who knows what, and I was sobbing. I didn't have tissue, but the man next to me pulled out a fresh roll of toilet paper and handed it to me! In a moment of clarity I thought, *God has such a sense of humor!* Then I continued to sob.

When the call came to come forward, I practically climbed over 10 rows of seats to get to the front to recommit myself to God. From that moment on, life was different. I closed my business, got a degree in religion, and for the past 10 years have been a youth pastor and school chaplain.

It's Holy Week—my favorite time. Today I had the honor of reminding 225 middle school students that Jesus loves them, died for them and forgives them.

—Patti

I want to hear from you, and I want to send you a
Bible in a modern translation. No charge. Please get in touch:

Greg@harvest.org.

Check out our ministry website:
www.harvest.org

and my personal website:
www.greglaurie.com

You can also read more lost boy and lost girl stories
and write your own story at:
http://blog.greglaurie.com/

Finally, a website that features my books:
www.allendavidbooks.com

God bless you!
Greg Laurie

ABOUT ELLEN VAUGHN

Ellen Vaughn is a *New York Times* bestselling author and inspirational speaker. Her recent books include *Time Peace, Radical Gratitude* and *It's All About Him*. The last, written for and with Denise Jackson, debuted at number 1 on the New York Times nonfiction list after its release in 2007. Vaughn's award-winning novels are *The Strand* and *Gideon's Torch*, which she coauthored with Chuck Colson. She collaborated with Colson on eight other nonfiction books, including ECPA Gold Medallion winners *Being the Body, The Body*, and *Kingdoms in Conflict*, which was re-released by Zondervan in 2007 as *God and Government*.

A former vice president of executive communications for Prison Fellowship, Vaughn speaks frequently at Christian retreats and conferences and has been featured at writers' seminars in the United States and Canada. Her articles have appeared in *Christianity Today, World* and *The Dallas Morning News*. Vaughn holds a Master of Arts from Georgetown University and a Bachelor of Arts from the University of Richmond.

Vaughn and her husband Lee live in the Washington, D.C., area with their energetic teenagers Emily, Haley and Walker.

WITH GRATITUDE

Thanks to the many people who helped this idea become a reality.

Ellen Vaughn, for your incredible skills as a writer and for keeping me on track.

Mark Ferjulian, for your patience and perseverance in seeing this through.

Carol Faulkner, John Collins and Paul Eaton, for your wonderful help and feedback.

Bill Greig III and Steve Lawson, for having the vision for this to begin with.

My best friend and wife, Cathe, for living all this with me and supporting me every step of the way. It's her story, too.

My sons, Jonathan and Christopher, and daughter-in-law, Brittany, for being the best kids one could hope for.

And to those who have been father figures to me over the years, including Chuck Smith, Keith Ritter, L. E. Romaine and, of course, Oscar Laurie.

Finally, to Billy Graham, a man who touched the world and my life in so many ways.

Other AllenDavid books
published by Kerygma
Publishing

The Great Compromise
For Every Season: Daily Devotions
Strengthening Your Marriage
Marriage Connections
Strengthening Your Faith
Deepening Your Faith
Living Out Your Faith
Dealing with Giants
Secrets to Spiritual Success
How to Know God
10 Things You Should Know About God and Life
For Every Season, vol. 2
The Greatest Stories Ever Told, vol.1
Making God Known
The Greatest Stories Ever Told, vol. 2
His Christmas Presence
Why God?
Better Than Happiness

 Visit: www.kerygmapublishing.com
www.allendavidbooks.com

LOST BOY

THE MOVIE

Find Out More By Visiting:

store.harvest.org

More Great Resources
from Regal

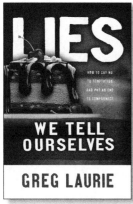

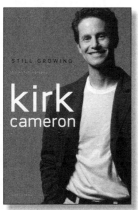
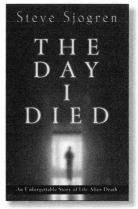